From Darkness
to Light

Tom Slone

5 05 440 0222
Tom @ Tom Slone . Com
Blessy Tom Slone

Revival Waves of Glory Books & Publishing
PO Box 596
Litchfield, IL 62056
www.revivalwavesofgloryministries.com

Paperback: 978-1717836915

Table of Contents

Foreword One v

Foreword Two.. ix

Preface xi

Chapter 1:
I Knew You Before You Were Born................................1

Chapter 2:
The Little Spirit Being Comes to Earth 23

Chapter 3:
First Steps...47

Chapter 4:
First Grade Trouble Begins..57

Chapter 5:
My Childhood: Gang Intimidation, Manipulation and Control 71

Chapter 6:
Moving to a New School and New Area –
Trouble Even Worse Than Before Begins......................89

Chapter 7:
Going to High School and Joining a New Gang............109

Chapter 8:
The Gangs Are All Here! The Beginning of Organized Crime...............135

Chapter 9:
The Last Week of Criminal Activity.............................147

Chapter 10:
The Beginning of a New Life Never Lived Before! 157

ABOUT THE AUTHOR...170

Foreword One

Tom Slone is a remarkable man with a remarkable story. His life from his earliest childhood seemed to be destined for tragedy. Growing up unwanted among the gangs of Chicago's Southside, Tom experienced ridicule and neglect, as well as physical, emotional, and sexual abuse at the hands of the very ones who should have protected him from those things. Forced to fight or die, Tom became a fighter, a gang leader and master in the occult practices of witchcraft. In his book, *From Darkness to Light*, Tom shares not only the circumstances, but also the hidden thoughts and feelings that transformed him from a wide-eyed little boy into a violent predator.

But Tom's story is not a tragedy; his story is one of redemption. This is the story of hopelessness transformed into hope, fear transformed into faith, and hatred transformed into love. It is the story of a broken man and of a miraculous God who reached into the utter darkness to rescue him and give him new life.

Years ago, we found a stray dog. His fur was a tangled mess; he was wild, aggressive, lacked manners, and clearly had learned to hunt to survive. The amazing thing about that dog is he seemed to remember what he had been rescued from and appreciated our home and family in a way other animals we have had did not. This occasionally can also be true of people. They remember what life was once like and seem to cherish more than others what they have been given in Christ. Jesus said, "He who has been forgiven much loves much." Tom is such a man. He remembers in vivid detail what his life was like without Jesus and has never lost that fresh gratitude and amazement at all Jesus has done for him.

Today, the violent gang-banger is long gone. Tom is a gentle, loving, and tenderhearted Pastor, teacher, evangelist, husband, father, and friend. He has a simple yet profound faith built upon a deep love of the scriptures and passion to walk in the ways of Jesus. His story is a living fulfillment of God's promise to transfer us out of the kingdom of darkness into the kingdom of His dear Son. He truly has gone from darkness to light.

- Dana Morey,

Evangelist and President, "A Light to the Nations"

Foreword Two

It has been my privilege to know Pastor Tom Slone for about 35 years. (Ordained 11-12-84. It will be 34 years on 11-12-18.)

I saw a man full of joy and optimism, and humble before God and His Son Jesus Christ.

As Tom shared his past on a tour through his old neighborhood where he was a gang leader in Chicago, I realized that his heart and mind had been renewed and transformed by the love and grace of our Lord Jesus Christ.

He has great compassion for all people and gives extended time and effort to those who come (seek or call) for ministry. He is like a rapid-fire machine gun equipped with the ammunition of revelation, wisdom, and prophesy. I'm so happy and thankful to see his life story reveal the truth of the gospel of God's love and grace through Jesus Christ to this generation.

God bless your (Heaven-sent) ministry to those who have failed over and over again. Praise God that real life begins through following and trusting Jesus with your life! (Just as it is right *now*!)

Philippians 1:6 (KJV), *"Being confident of this very thing, that **He** which hath begun a good work in you will perform it until the day of Jesus Christ,"*

and

Mark 9:23 (KJV), *"If thou canst believe, **all** things are possible **to him** that **believeth**."*

- Reverend Jim Haligas,

Pastor, Believers Prayer Fellowship Church

Glen Ellyn, IL

Preface

This book documents the story of my life from before I was born up until the time I was taken to Heaven and had a supernatural encounter with God on March 4, 1979. It is at this time that God wanted me to write about my experiences and publish this book. My extreme transformation from Satanism, being involved in organized crime and living my life as a gang leader, to becoming a follower of Jesus Christ, means God can save anyone.

God wants to touch the lives of many people supernaturally through the testimony He has given me. I was born into a disadvantaged family of gang members on the South Side of Chicago and suffered abuse from the beginning of my life – only to be rescued and mentored by a powerful Satanic high priest. I became a very powerful sorcerer and as mean as a junkyard dog, quickly rising to become a gang leader and exact revenge on the people who had hurt me or would cross me.

Part of the perspective given in this book includes what God showed me was taking place in the spiritual realm before we came to Earth and while we are living on Earth. The insights He showed me explain how the good and evil forces work to influence and at times control our lives.

Since choosing to accept Jesus Christ and to serve Him, I have graduated from *Christ for the Nations Institute* and traveled the world preaching, teaching, and testifying the good news of Jesus Christ. For many years I was asked to write the story of my life but was never released to do it. I went from being a gang leader to speaking and ministering in a variety of churches, and at one point I felt like many churches acted just like a bunch of gangs, with all their doctrinal and theological differences.

Today is a new day. There is a hunger and openness to supernatural heavenly encounters and revelations, and people in general are ready to learn deeper things from God.

I wanted to thank my family, my wife, Dana, Karman and the whole Morey family, and many other people who have believed in me and supported the work of God in my life.

Chapter 1:
I Knew You Before You Were Born

*"Before I formed thee in the belly I knew thee; and before thou camest forth out of the womb I sanctified thee, **and** I ordained thee a prophet unto the nations."* Jeremiah 1:5, King James Version (KJV)

The phrase *"I knew you before you were in your mother's womb"* means "we had a relationship before you came to Earth."

There was an eternal day eons ago when all the light beings came together, enjoying the heart of the Father, the depths of His wonderful love, and the delights of the heavenly realms. We were similar to angelic beings – full of energy, happiness, and excitement, playing in the wonderful rainbow waters of light and life, enjoying the sweetness, the loving embrace and the gentle movements of the winds, and the caressing, loving expressions of the fatherhood and divine motherhood of God. We were oblivious to the future, just knowing that we were precious in His sight and that His thoughts were like the sands of the seashore for each one of us. We so loved our times together as friends, and because of the supernatural state of the world itself, we were able to enjoy and know the Father, so holy and divine with His feminine heart. For us, the supreme heavenly realms were places to enjoy, play, and have communication with our friends. Some heavenly friends would even be connected to us in the future, so on that day when we would have met again on Earth, we would say, *It seems like we've met before.*

In those supernatural realms created by Father God, we would dance, sing, be entertained, and enjoy all the wonderful, exciting pathways and amazing portals that took us wherever we liked in the universes of the Creator's love, protection, kindness, and tenderness. Wherever we went, we always felt that we were light beings of love. The purity was so good, the excitement was so fantastic, and the memory of it was so profound. We all loved the special foods and drinks of light, and every created thing was made of light and alive in its own special way. The communication we experienced was beyond words and natural knowledge. It was so special because we communicated through knowing inside of ourselves what was really being conveyed, and in the same manner we responded back to each other via this spiritual, indescribable inner communication. Understanding and comprehending exactly what was being communicated was so pure and enjoyable.

We had lots of good times when we existed before the beginning of time with Father God; we had each other as friends, along with angelic friends who would later become our guardians in our future earthly missions. We used to talk together and wonder about our future missions on Earth, but really, we had no idea what they would be like. We would talk to the Father about our future in the earthly world where we would become changed into another form of being, created in His image. We were told that being sent into that world would lead us to receive the most fantastic, wonderful Entity into our hearts and lives: Jesus Christ, the resurrected King of Kings and Lord of Lords. We would see parts of our future on Earth, talk with one another about the images we saw and the feelings, emotions and expressions we experienced, and try to comprehend the meaning of these future events. Even when we were contemplating our future earthly missions with the Father, He would assure us that what He began, He would surely finish and bring to completion through His Precious Son.

We were all excited about the time when we would be placed inside a woman's womb and then become a human being. We could not comprehend or understand these things fully, yet we eagerly awaited our turn to go. The meaning of living a new life on Earth as a human being was beyond us because we lived in such a fantastic, magical world where anything we wanted was pure and was given to us. All of our friends seemed to always be with us, and so we never even considered being apart. The angels enjoyed playing with us, and they communicated and talked with us whenever we wanted. All we knew and understood in our life before the beginning of time with Father God was love in all of its expressions, which was greater than any man, woman, a mother, or a father on Earth could give. We lived experiencing His perfect love in its purest form. We would play in the trees, and whatever images we saw would transport us into that reality, so we constantly tapped into endless things in the heavenly realms that were so good, fun, and enjoyable. All along we were wondering and thinking together about the future, just like little children. We couldn't wait to come to the place called Earth and begin exploring and experiencing life as human beings. We thought Earth would be a wonderful place – even though there was talk going around that it would not be easy for us to live and grow up on Earth. Compared to our blissful existence in the heavenly realms with Father God, we could not comprehend or even think of the meaning of danger and other things that would happen on Earth because of the fall of man. We just wanted to do whatever our loving Father asked of us. It was so exciting to serve Him while at the same time dwelling within the loving, feminine part of Him, and therefore we all wanted to stay close to Him, like children would want to stay near their mother. We were told that when being sent on our earthly missions, we would at first be very comfortable inside our mothers' wombs, and our guardian angels would go with us. We were even told that some of us would not make it through the process and would be sent back to the heavenly places and into the arms of the loving Creator. We would return in a different form, and that form would be of a man, the mankind and womankind of Earth, created in the image and likeness of God: spirit, heart, soul, and body.

We were all excited as we would play in the trees, talk to the animals, walk, float, and fly. We were ecstatic to come to Earth, thinking it was just another new joyous adventure, and never thought we would ever lose everything that we had ever known. In our existence with the Creator, we could enjoy, play, explore, and have an adventure in all the worlds-within-worlds of our Creator and our dear heavenly Father. We loved to see His delightful face that expressed enjoyment of how much His creations so loved to please Him in any way. When looking at other light beings and how they were similar to the angelic creatures, we could never dream of what we would become on Earth.

...Then the Adventure Began

We remembered the time when the Father started physical creation. We all shouted in triumph when it began, and we felt safe even when the fall of Heylel[1] came. We could not fathom how Lucifer and those that followed him from the ranks and tribes of angels could want to leave such wonder and bliss, walk away, and please themselves, rather than want to please the Father. Even then, we were happy, comfortable, and completely protected from the fallen beings and lived in the light of the heavenly realms, without the knowledge of what the night was like, or the need of any sleep. All of our experiences were exciting, adventurous, enjoyable, and went on for what seemed like eternity – until the time came when the Father said to one of us, *"Are you ready to go to that planet called Earth, be born of a woman, and fulfill your mission? I'm going to tell you what your mission is, and then I'm going to hide it on the scroll of your heart. I will engrave it in you, so that when you are there, you will feel like you came from somewhere and you have a purpose to be there, to fulfill something that you sense deep inside of you, especially when you are young. Even as a little child, you will know and feel what you're supposed to do, and it will rise up inside of you. It will*

---

[1] The first Angel created by God. Dictionary of the Bible has the original name as 'helēl (helāl) ben shachar.' The KJV Bible calls him Lucifer, Son of the Morning or Venus.

communicate with you, and I will send My angels and guardians to protect you and to make it come to pass, and then you will come to the fullness of age. As you mature and grow, a time will come when you receive My Son into your heart, become like Him, and completely fulfill your mission on Earth."

We were always so excited and we wanted to do whatever the Creator said. We laughed about the stories He told us regarding ourselves in the future, and joked about them, yet did not really know anything about our future missions on Earth as human beings. It seemed funny to us, but we enjoyed the Creator's love and all those wonderful, beautiful things of the heavenly realms. It seemed to us that everything would be the same no matter what He said; that everything would look wonderful and lovely, including the beautiful beings that we would meet. We had no idea of how the realms would change for us, what a physical dimension was like, and how we would experience life on Earth. We were overjoyed to continue to get ready for our earthly missions. So, day went to day, age to age, and eternity to eternity. We enjoyed the wonderful life in the eternal worlds with Father God, dwelled in the feminine realms and angelic realms within our

Creator, spent our time dancing, jumping and sliding, and adored the wonderful rainbows within the beautiful stones in the waters of life and the skies within.

Our Heavenly Father created something so wonderful and so beautiful: the gardens, the trees, the beautiful creatures of all kinds, and everything that was created was alive. We would talk to the clouds, the skies, the water, the trees, the animals, and the divine angelic beings. We enjoyed the music, the entertaining shows and performances of other beings, and the things and cultures of the heavenly realms. We never thought that we could be separated in any way from such wonder and love, even though we were told that at some point we were to receive His Son Jesus Christ into our lives. We couldn't wait to receive Jesus Christ, but we were told it had to happen while we were on Earth. We had to receive the sacrifice through what Jesus Christ did on the cross and through His blood, so that we could become an immortal new creation that would eternally live with Father God in the heavenly realms with a greater enjoyment than ever before.

Then the adventure began when, one after another, we went to Earth. And we were all so happy to go and do the Father's will, not even knowing what home we would be placed in, or what parents we would be joined to. Multimillions of beings accepted the Father's will and left for Earth to fulfill their missions. Once the soul has been joined to physical matter, you bear the image and likeness of Father God, the Son of God, Jesus Christ, and the Holy Spirit. You become a different type of a fallen creation – a triune being made up of spirit, soul, and body – no matter what circumstances or demons were involved to cause the parents to come together and conceive: with or without love, marriage, or being romantically joined together. You become a citizen of Earth, and later, when you receive Jesus Christ, you again become a citizen of the heavenly bliss and the worlds of the Creator. Your earthly mission is to learn to rule and reign with Him, seated at His right hand forever as special, mature, trained sons and daughters of God the Father, the Son, and the Holy Spirit. This whole process brings you back to Father God, and one day you finally get reunited with your guardians and angelic beings, your old friends, and all the tribes of the Heavens – the great family who loves you more than anyone on Earth ever could.

Meanwhile in a Place Far, Far Away...

*"For we wrestle not against flesh and blood, but against principalities, against powers, against the rulers of the darkness of this world, against spiritual wickedness in high **places**."* Ephesians 6:12

The rulers of darkness have regular meetings with all the demons to discuss and set the assignments that cause great harm, misery, suffering, and pain to the citizens of Earth. And, as most of us already know, people can actually end up having a difficult physical life and wind up in the realms of hell because of all the demonic powers they served while on Earth through their choices, rationalizations, and justifications. Outside of fantasy or fiction, most humans would never ever think that there was a war between invisible kingdoms, and that they got right in the middle of it the moment they were conceived. God, however, never wanted it like that. He wanted all humans to live with Him forever and enjoy all the things that the Creator had planned for them during

11

eternity – wonderful things that the eye has not seen. These are the beautiful things the Father has planned for those who love Him. The Earth is only a shadow of things to come; the best times you could ever have on this planet are just a poor imitation of what you can have in the heavenly dimensions. During our life on Earth, Father God has given us good things to experience, like waking up to the beautiful mornings, seeing the sun rise or set, admiring the beauty of nature, the animals, the birds of the sky, the creatures of the sea – the countless species within His creation and how they communicate with one another. We can enjoy all kinds of fruits and vegetables, as well as other types of food available to us. He has given us more than enough to feed everyone on this planet, and then some; however, there is lack and misery for many because of the invisible war. Life on Earth is an experience and opportunity to come to know Him and to choose eternal life with Him.

*"And God said, let there be lights in the firmament of the heaven to **divide the day from the night**; and let them be for signs, and for seasons, and for days, and years..."*
Genesis 1:14, King James Version (KJV)

"(He) commandeth the sun, and it riseth not; and sealeth up the stars. (He) alone spreadeth out the heavens, and treadeth upon the waves of the sea. (He) maketh Arcturus, Orion, and Pleiades, and the chambers of the south." Job 9:7-9, King James Version (KJV)

"Canst thou bind the sweet influences of Pleiades, or loose the bands of Orion? Canst thou bring forth Mazzaroth in his season? Or canst thou guide Arcturus (the Great Bear) *with his sons?"* Job 38:31-32, King James Version (KJV)

The moon, the sun, the zodiacs, and the massive beings under those signs, as well as the demons, are joined together into the meeting places that are active every moment of every single day and night – watching for the time when a person is conceived on Earth. The demons of the father and mother to be are joined together for diabolical programming plans, using councils and holding meetings, discussing how to corrupt, distort, kill, or maim.

13

The hierarchy of demonic beings continually discusses plans and assignments for each time when a subject is born, for thousands of years, according to the family status in the world, their education, work or employment, mental capabilities, talents or gifts, and abilities of each family line, nationality, culture, and religion. Depending on possible strategic outcomes, demons constantly strategize and implement additional diabolical ways to bring over what they want for people in the world. Every plan is developed in accordance with each human being and how they fit or do not fit into society or culture, so that they could eventually become channels for the demons. With willing participants, the demons begin to express what they want and then make people think it was their own thoughts and ideas; thus, their minds, hearts, souls, and lives as humans are fully programmed and conditioned.

At some point, all humans begin to believe to some extent that no one can tell them what they can or can't do. There is where the deception lies, and this is how the demonic beings get seeded into someone and establish control over their entire life. However, according to the Bible, Jesus said that we have power over all satanic forces of the enemy.

"Behold, I give unto you power to tread on serpents and scorpions, and over all the power of the enemy: and nothing shall by any means hurt you." Luke 10:19

God tells us to take every thought captive; that's how we do it – by recognizing what's going on in our minds. Then we decide and rationalize how we are going to use our will, which is one of the most powerful weapons in the universe. We either allow the evil forces to control us and make us think that we're thinking our own thoughts, or we choose to think the good things. Our best and most fantastic thoughts, pictures, and words come from God and His angelic beings and reinforce our connection with them. The evil thoughts, pictures, and words come from the enemy and his demons through our family lines to reinforce our connection with them. We are connected to both the heavenly realms and the demonic realms and are constantly being pulled back and forth in the invisible war.

We Were Never Alone

The angels and the guardians, however, have their meetings as well. An eternity before I came to Earth, there was a meeting that went on continuously concerning billions of people on this planet. My guardians, warriors, those that would protect and watch over me, and the angels that would write down the story of my life and help me develop the supernatural giftings that would be sent with me, got together in one place. Some of them were angels that would be in charge of special protection, and so they discussed their strategy by looking at all that would happen in the slipstream – the dimension where time is known, yet outside of eternity. This is where they could in detail look at every single thing that would ever happen, every thought that I would think, every word that I would say, all that would go in my heart, and how the demonic powers would be communicating to me all the things that they wanted for my life on Earth.

However, a greater plan from Father God would be to see to it that my life would turn into a fantastic, great victory no matter what would take place; that I would have help from the angels who would work in and through me to make sure that I would come to know the Father God, Jesus Christ, and His Son in my lifetime on Earth. The angels would continue helping me to fulfill my missions and eventually be used in one of the most remarkable moves of God in human history – *the outpouring of His Spirit upon all flesh.*

"And it shall come to pass afterward, that I will pour out my spirit upon all flesh; and your sons and your daughters shall prophesy, your old men shall dream dreams, your young men shall see visions..." Joel 2:28, King James Version (KJV)

"But this is that which was spoken by the prophet Joel; And it shall come to pass in the last days, saith God, I will pour out of my Spirit upon all flesh: and your sons and your daughters shall prophesy, and your young men shall see visions, and your old men shall dream dreams..." Acts 2:16-17, King James Version (KJV)

What a wonderful thing God the Father, His Son, and His Spirit have provided for each individual who comes to Earth! Just think about that – everyone has the ability to come back into a relationship with Him through His Son! Through the special blood sacrifice of Jesus, anyone can receive life, enter into Heaven forever, and enjoy eternal bliss.

During those strategic planning meetings, the angels and guardians would talk about how the enemy's plans would come to pass, then how God would intercept every evil thing through His angels and His Word, and what He would speak to me and through me. The heavenly team would discuss how He would allow me to have a great victory in my life and overcome all things the enemy threw at me. The angels and guardians explained to one another what would take place while I was inside my mother's womb, and how they would be able to know what was going on with me at that specific time.

They already knew I would have a disease at the beginning of my life that would almost kill me. Because of the curses that came down to me from my family line, I would be sick a lot in my younger days, from being born premature and having underdeveloped body parts and other weaknesses. They were also aware that the demons were scheming to destroy me and channel their energy through my parents. These demons would plan their attack, but the angels knew that the Father had His own miraculous ways of bringing me out of every horrible thing that I would ever encounter.

One of the most amazing things about being part of God's creation is that no matter the circumstances or situations, God wants all of us to be overcomers of all things, triumphant over all things; but most of all, He wants us to be with Him in eternity. We are all His children, and He loves us always – no matter what we do or go through. God's desire is that we would come into a reality of knowing Him and wanting to be with Him forever.

"The eye has not seen neither has the ear heard what God has prepared for those that love Him."

1 Corinthians 2:9

"And we love Him because He first loved us."

1 John 4:19

So, the angels discussed what was going to take place in my life; and they knew exactly how the enemy was purposefully planning to kill me, or make me sick, or harm me in many ways – physically, emotionally, but most of all spiritually. They talked about how they were going to come against those demons and spirits that would be there during every moment or second of my life – through my thoughts, feelings, desires, attitudes, dreams, visions, supernatural experiences, and through the various degradations of darkness. They shared with one another precisely how they were going to intercept in between those forces and powers, and perform acts that even in the natural world would cause complete defeat to the enemy's forces.

I was shown that this process was the same for every single human ever born. The warriors of Heaven had their swords of light and power, and they could not wait to put them to work and destroy the forces of darkness in people's lives. For my life, they also had to consider what my parents were thinking and talking about; how they were channeling the demonic powers, and how the relatives were going to react to those demonic powers. Strategies were made and perfected, for the enemy would not know what the angelic powers from Heaven were going to do. The angels always worked tirelessly to bring God's will into every human being's life on Earth because of the Creator's great love for us.

The angels held their meetings in the multimillions of war rooms, which showed them all the levels and layers of the physical world, the demonic world, the spirit and soul of the individual and, of course, the angelic world. Nothing is ever missed, and they see it all – even our minds, souls, and hearts, as well as thoughts that are sent as fiery arrows from the enemy. They even see what goes on in the mind of an individual as they reason, understand, and think before words are spoken. The angels can imagine what's on your mind, and they have access to the memories from all the spiritual dimensions, used by the enemy to implant thoughts into the minds of human beings. A good example of a memory from the spiritual dimensions would be an idea of reincarnation – where individuals supposedly have visions of a prior life that come from the enemy. Those memories are a mixture of past human memories and connections to spiritual forces from the second heaven that are channeling thoughts into the heads of human beings.

With all this knowledge and access to information, the angels know how to execute the plan with perfection because they can map out everything even before someone comes into this world. The angels know from the beginning to the end everything that the enemy will do and how humans will respond – and that goes for every single person born on Earth. Even after birth, when humans learn to walk and live in this realm, the angels know what should happen in the physical plane and what their special assignments will be. Angels are already assigned to protect, love, and help humans according to God's plan made in Heaven. After all, each one of us is an overcomer in the making.

"To him that overcometh will I grant to sit with Me in My throne, even as I also overcame, and am set down with My Father in His throne." Revelation 3:21, King James Version (KJV)

Chapter 2:
The Little Spirit Being
Comes to Earth

"Behold, I was shapen in iniquity, and in sin did my mother conceive me." Psalm 51:5, King James Version (KJV)

We are sent to Earth to be born, grow up, attend school, learn life's lessons, and find Jesus Christ. We are to come to know Him intimately and to understand that He came to bring us back to Heaven through His sacrifice on the cross, so we can have eternal life forever with the Father.

Whenever a couple comes together and creates a child, the conception takes place, and a little spirit is sent to Earth with a guardian angel (and other angels assigned to protect them, depending on the gifts and callings of God for this particular individual). The little spirit being takes on flesh and forms in the belly of the mother in the image and likeness of the Creator. Once the little spirit being who dwelled with God the Father takes on human form, all memory of their prior existence is lost. Even before the baby is born, he or she is comfortable in the womb and gets to share the emotions and feelings of his mother. The baby can feel whatever she goes through, even when the enemy is there, interacting or inflicting damage. After conception, the spirit is put into the flesh that begins to form, and the baby begins to grow and receive the nurture that flows through the mother, the care of the angels that are with them, or the demons that are coming against them through negative feelings and energy.

In my case, my mother had emotional problems because of the passing of my grandmother on my father's side. The emotional distress made her go into premature labor and, in turn, caused me a ton of problems when I was born. This made the demons so happy! If they managed to stop my little spirit from developing and being born as a human being in the image and likeness of God, my life would have ended before it even started. I would have not been allowed to live out my life and fulfill God's plan, but instead I would have been sent back to Heaven into the Father's loving arms and His limitless worlds.

So even while I was in my mother's womb, I was already feeling rejection from the thoughts coming from her. She was distressed because she wasn't married yet, and on top of that she had plenty of problems with her emotions and thoughts. These were transferred to me, and I unintentionally took on all of my mother's guilt; thus, I would feel it since I was inside her womb. It was destined to be a complicated birth because my mother was grieving for the loss of my grandmother.

The angels tried to get involved and give comfort, strength, and help by sending divine energy to aid me and by making me feel good things while I swam inside my mother's womb. I could feel that there was nothing to hold on to in my world other than the energy that I was being given. There were no memories of the future physical Earth during that stage, and I wasn't able to relate to the things I would hear about my coming life.

My grandmother used to tap into the occult world, which allowed those spirits to begin waiting, strategizing, and planning on how to afflict me with the evil things from the spiritual dimension known as *"the second heaven"*. The curse came through my father that caused me to eventually grow up, become a sorcerer, and hurt many people in the world.

One of the curses given to me was an affliction to the eyes and partial blindness so that I would grow up handicapped. Since I was not formed correctly during my mother's pregnancy, the enemy took it as an opportunity to come in and affect me with different illnesses like anemia, which caused me to be sick for the most of my young life.

What the demons really wanted to do was to kill me even before I was born, but since that was not possible, they gave me a lot of diseases to torment me. The demons knew that the angels could not interfere with what they were going to do to me because of the curses from my family lines. However, the demons still made a lot of alternative plans – just in case the first several plans did not work to the degree that was necessary to control and guide my life for their purposes.

The angels were already informed about the demonic plans and what was really going on. They already knew based on the war room meetings before I came to Earth that all things would work out for good in spite of what the enemy would try to plan for my life. My entire existence on Earth would seem to be in jeopardy, but from the angels' standpoint, they were going to protect me. They were going to make sure there would be a fight with the warring angels against the demonic angels, because the Father already said I would one day be His own. It was already shown to them that I would come to the saving knowledge of Jesus Christ. No matter what I went through, God the Father, Jesus the Son, and the Holy Spirit would specifically look after me, as He did after any and all children who were ever born into this world.

"Keep me as the apple of Your eye, hide me under the shadow of Your wings from the wicked that oppress me, from my deadly enemies who surround me."

Psalm 17:8-9

I was born under the Zodiac sign Leo, the sun sign. It was a premature birth, happening two months early. I was born with the positive and negative characteristics, including those that the demons had planned for me. Everything was included in my being, written in my palms, seen in my eyes, on the bottom of my feet, in the chakras, auras, and energies that were communicating inside and outside of me. The same thing happens with all the children who are born into the world.

Born on the South Side

I was born into a poor family – a labor family living in an area where gangs and organized crime were a part of life, where life and death were dealt with on a daily basis. Life in the inner city, on the South Side of Chicago, would be very difficult for anybody. Songs have been written about how terrible these places are, for the demons want everyone to know about the South Side of Chicago and how people are bad there – like that *"bad, bad Leroy Brown, the worst man in the whole town, meaner than a junkyard dog."*[1] That's the kind of area that I was born in, where most of the humans faced very difficult situations growing up. The demons of lack and deficiency allowed the spirit of greed to rule the families and conquer the human spirits. The people would try to find any possible way to make money, like stealing, selling goods, gambling, and all other sorts of things. So, because of lack and poverty, the demons prepared the way for criminal activity and enterprises that ended up ruling the area.

On my mother's side, her dad had two wives at the same time, twenty-something children, and dozens of grandchildren. My grandfather was a cab driver, played cards and bet on horses, didn't have enough money to support the family, and was an alcoholic and a very violent man overall. With all those children and grandchildren, it was impossible to keep track of them, and the children would leave to escape the violence, growing into robbers and thieves. Instead of going grocery shopping to bring food home to the family, the children would go out and steal food to put on the table. Even the 7-year-old and 8-year-old children joined together with

---

[1] "Bad, Bad Leroy Brown" is a song written by American folk rock singer Jim Croce and released as part of his 1973 album *Life and Times*.

their older siblings, cousins, uncles, and friends. My family was like a gang of its own, and at about the age of 11, I remember going with them to rob cars and trains. My family was full of all sorts of evil, incest of all kinds, and, as most people in modern-day America would say, it was a very dysfunctional family altogether.

When I was born, they all loved me, just like most families do. They smothered me with love and kisses, and I enjoyed all of it. Family members visited us as I grew up, and my mother took good care of me despite the grief she was feeling because of the death, of her husband's mother. My parents got married quickly just before having me and now, being married, they needed to get a place to live, whereas before they lived together in an apartment that belonged to my father's parents.

The angels were excited because I made it through the birth process, even though it was very difficult. Now they had to keep me alive and fight the demons that would try to snuff out my life and cause me to go back to Heaven before the age of accountability. The demons knew that they had lost the initial battle, so they went back to their schemes and plans to figure out another way to kill me since they couldn't see what the angels were about to do or how they would do it. The demons do not have war rooms, information, or insight that are given to the angels of Heaven to help the humans on Earth with the divine plans of God the Father, Jesus the Son, and the Holy Spirit.

*"For I know the thoughts that I think toward you, saith the Lord, thoughts of peace, and not of evil, to give you an **expected end**."*

Jeremiah 29:11, King James Version (KJV)

Since I survived the birth process, the demons had to create another plan to kill me. They already planted a disease in me, and they intended for it to kill me before my first birthday. They also caused a lot of stress to my mother, such as the tension due to the lack of financial capability to take care of me. The family did what they could; they gave clothes and things for me, but for a short period time I had to sleep inside a dresser drawer until they found something better for me to sleep in. As long as I was loved and comforted, and my needs were taken care of, I was happy, just like all those little babies.

Let the Battle Commence

My mother and father did not know, nor could they understand, the spiritual battle that took place before I was born. I was conceived outside of marriage; therefore, it opened the door to evil, or, as the Bible explains it, a curse came upon the child through the father's DNA.

In the spiritual dimension, the demons, in their regular fashion, take orders from their kings and princes to figure out ways to bring curses to the children that are born on Earth. The demons care nothing about how innocent the child is if the parents sinned and opened the door to them through things that the Bible calls sin. This is when curses can enter a person's life to kill or inflict pain, trauma, suffering, confusion, mind blocks, mental disorders, wedges between family members, and all sorts of evil. This is also when the spiritual occult gifts are imparted based on a person's family line, but those gifts come with torments.

On the other hand, when God the Father gives gifts, there is never any torment associated with it – only spiritual goodness from Heaven and His kingdom. However, from the demonic standpoint, when a child is born outside of marriage, or even conceived outside of marriage, the Bible says that a curse will follow that child to the fourth generation, for *"I the Lord your God am a jealous God"* (Exodus 20:5).

In other words, He wants us to only follow His ways for our own good – so we can overcome all things for His pleasure and glory. The next few verses of this book in the Bible talk about how God is forgiving, but will by no means clear the guilty.

"(He is) *keeping mercy for thousands, forgiving iniquity and transgression and sin, by no means clearing the guilty, visiting the iniquity of the fathers upon the children and the children's children to the third and the fourth generation."* Exodus 34:7

It says here that the Lord is *"keeping mercy for thousands"*, which means He is capable of maintaining love for billions of people and willing to forgive evil and continuous wrongdoing; however, He will by no means clear the guilty. Therefore, you cannot get over on God, for He knows it all. Iniquity opens the doors for the demons of the fathers to put curses upon the children and the children's children, unto the third and fourth generation. Examples of these are diseases that people become afflicted with because of what their parents did before they were conceived, for the parents went out past the protective fence that God had set up.

I want to make this very clear, since all humans go past the guidelines and the laws that God has set up. Once a parent sins, it opens the door for the demons to come in and afflict the babies, even as they grow into adults, until someone leads them to accept Jesus into their lives and makes them aware that He can set them free. They become free on the inside, once He applies His sacrifice, and they know it. However, that doesn't mean that they will be released from their sicknesses or diseases, unless the Spirit of God begins to heal them. God desires that all people would be healed, but the time of the healing only comes whenever He chooses.

I almost died before my first birthday. Where did that curse come from? All the demons know why children are born with various curses that cause them to have issues with all kinds of sicknesses throughout their entire lives. Some are deformed, born in twisted ways, have damaged organs or missing body parts, and twins are sometimes stuck together and need surgical separation. Since all that God does is good, it is the enemy and demonic forces from the spiritual world that are involved in corrupting the DNA and causing sickness and even death in people. Parents do not really know what they are doing when they make sinful choices and go past the guidelines and laws of God, and that's why the powers of darkness rule this planet up to this day. However, *God is going to change that soon.*

This war between the angels and demons goes on every single day, and billions of people living on Earth don't realize the plans and schemes of the enemy while babies are born and families grow. If only their eyes were opened, like with some who have looked into the spiritual dimensions just moments before death! There is a real world beyond this one, and it is full of demons and angels. When some people are passing, Jesus visits them, and they are able to see the reality of what goes on behind the scenes.

With that said, God knew about the invisible war between good and evil from the very beginning and wanted to protect people from curses, and that's why

He told us about blessings and curses in the Old Testament; and then Jesus Christ is revealed to us in the New Testament to completely remove the curse of the Law.

The reason why Jesus acts differently than the God of the Old Testament is because He became the supreme sacrifice. It was through His blood and His sacrifice on the cross that all curses were broken off of us. Therefore, justice prevailed, and the demons no longer had the right to afflict those humans who received His supreme sacrifice on the cross. All their evil thoughts and the bad things they did in their lives were nailed to the cross. Their thoughts, emotions, passions, mind pictures, images, and memories were all spiritual things that came from the spiritual world and were connected to the occult world. This entire process is called *"the Wheel"*. Like spokes on a bicycle wheel, our lives are tied to our souls, which represents our will – the most powerful weapon we can use. We have to choose to say "yes" or "no", to open or close the door to God the Father, Jesus the Son, the Holy Spirit, or the demons and spirits of the demonic world. The battles that we face are the result of what our fathers and mothers did when they were younger, and what their fathers and mothers did, and so on throughout the past generations. The cycles continue in everyone's life, with different kinds of afflictions and curses that follow what people did in their hearts and thoughts, or what they chose to do physically. Bad thoughts, emotions, attitudes, imaginations, music, and other things create portals, opening up ways and doors for the demons, the principalities, the powers, the rulers of darkness, and the spiritual wickedness in high places to afflict humans. Jesus deals with these things, giving us the power to conquer and rule over all spiritual powers.

"Behold, I give you the authority to trample on serpents and scorpions, and over all the power of the enemy..."
Luke 10:19

This refers to serpents as deceptive spirits and scorpions as tormenting spirits. You can have power over all of the enemy's forces, and nothing shall, by any means, hurt you. When you choose to listen to what Jesus is talking about and you do what He says, then He automatically starts cutting off your enemies. Every single one of us has an eternal foe that hates us and wants to inflict curses, sickness and even death. There were a lot of things that were not formed correctly in my body, such as my lungs, eyes, immune system, and blood, which were critical for my survival. The demons wanted to kill me and stop the plan that God had for me on this Earth. During the first year of my life, it was a very close fight for who would succeed – the demons in killing me or the angels of God in saving me.

The angels fought with God's power. They drew their swords and jumped right into battle because God had other plans for me. I was going to become an overcomer and share my faith and God's Word with many people. I was going to receive Jesus one day and the wonderful things that He did for me, and God was going to completely turn my life around for His honor and glory.

Living in Hell on the Way to Heaven

Of course, after my birth my mother was terrified. She just brought me into the world, and now the doctors were telling her that I might not live. They advised her that I would have to be put into an incubator, and on top of that, that I might not grow right because there were major things wrong with my body parts. Since she was already feeling so much guilt for conceiving me before marriage, all of this horrible news was causing her additional pain and distress. The demons were making the most of the opportunity to play on her guilt, convincing her that it was all her fault and that she was the one who caused me to be in such a terrible state. The deceptive spirits were working overtime to keep her feeling guilty and in continual suffering. Even so, God had a plan for her. One day, she would be released from the feelings of guilt and condemnation for conceiving a child before getting married.

When my mother originally told my father that she was pregnant, he got very upset. He thought about all the things that they needed to do, including getting married because of the pregnancy. They did not want a child and were not prepared for it, so when I was conceived, the rejection that came from the demons was pointed towards me. The demons made me feel like I did not belong, that I was not wanted, even while I was still inside my mother's womb. The demons were able to twist the normal DNA and include a curse because of my parents' sin of conceiving a child outside of marriage.

Then there was the problem of not having adequate finances to start a family. My parents were concerned about how they were going to take care of me. They lived with my father's parents and needed to get their own place; this obviously caused a lot of pressure. The fear instilled by the demons was very strong because my parents were guilty and deserving of the curse. They had no education. My father and his friends were involved in the neighborhood gangs. I was born in one of the worst places to live – on the South Side of Chicago. I was raised in the worst part of town, which meant I would grow up meaner than a junkyard dog. I had experienced the most severe rejection – the one that came from both my mother *and* my father who hated me and never wanted me. I hated my life as I was growing up because of the rejection, suffering, sicknesses, beatings, bruises, and pain that I went through.

God says when you follow Him, you will have everything you need, and more; an abundant life. But the atmosphere of my home was flooded with demons and the fears that my parents transferred to me. Every home has either a heavenly or a hellish atmosphere. The more hell that you have in the atmosphere of your home, the more the family feels the weight of the curse. Nevertheless, there is a better way to live. As I write this book, I know that I am also teaching you how to accomplish that. It's not just a story of my life, since the principles outlined here will work in many people's lives and potentially change them for the better.

"For God so loved the world that he gave his only begotten Son, that whosoever believeth in him should not perish, but have everlasting life. For God sent not his Son into the world to condemn the world; but that the world through him might be saved."

John 3:16-17, King James Version (KJV)

Not only can we enter into His Kingdom, which is in Heaven, and be with Him forever, but we can also have the curses removed from us forever as we apply what He did to our lives. Although it may take a whole lifetime to get rid of these curses, I can verify that God will work in our lives until we leave this Earth.

I also had to go through all the normal things that a child goes through during their upbringing. People who visited us at our home, both family friends and random acquaintances, made comparisons of whether I looked like certain members of our family or behaved like them. There were some who said I looked like my father, with his gestures and other behaviors. At the same time, the demons were playing with my father's mind, causing him to feel hatred towards me since my birth. The reason for his hatred is unknown to me to this day. Obviously, he did not want a child because he had other plans for his life. My parents got married before I was born only to make it look right, so that the people who would look upon them would be appeased. They didn't want to be judged by their friends and relatives. They thought people would think that it was okay for them to have a baby together because they were married. But the demons did not look at it that way. I was still conceived outside of marriage, and the demons had rights, by laws of the supernatural courts, to come against me and try to kill me.

However, the angels of the living God would come to empower me and help me fight off the demons from my father's side. For God said to the angels, *"This child is going to be a testimony of My Kingdom, of what I can do with the human race. Through My power I will set him free, and through My Son's blood I will break those curses off of his life. Once he comes to Jesus Christ, My warring angels will stand with him throughout his life to break every spell, every curse, every enemy's hack out of his life, and he will crush the evil forces that once ruled his life; he will conquer all the forces of darkness that plagued him. He will forgive all those people that hurt or bruised him in the atmosphere of his home because of the evil schemes of the demons, the envies and jealousies of the friends of his parents, and the evil eye of the people within the occult world."*

The angels knew that I would have a very difficult life. But they were also aware that I would stand in the spirit and power of Elijah and one day go all over the world to proclaim that Jesus can set anyone free. As I would speak, the power of the living God would fall upon people and break the curses off of them. Those curses would follow them due to the poor choices of their family members, peers, friends, and relatives through the demonic atmospheres because the demons hated every human being from the start and loved no one at any time.

"The thief cometh not, but for to steal, and to kill, and to destroy: I am come that they might have life, and that they might have it more abundantly."

John 10:10, King James Version (KJV)

The purpose of the demonic forces is to steal, or rob, to kill, or annihilate, and to destroy, or completely ruin your life. But the Father and the Son say, *"Follow My way, and We guarantee that you will have Our kind of life in a greater abundance than you have ever dreamed of."* How wonderful God's plans are for us – to make us overcomers over all the darkness in our lives!

When I was an infant, my parents tried to make me as comfortable as possible –even when I was sleeping in my little dresser drawer bed. They did not know that I slept soundly because I was listening to the songs of the angels. Those heavenly beings ministered love and the presence of God to me as I grew up from an infant into a toddler. They were always fighting for my life, even from the very beginning. I started off in a very difficult situation, being born on the South Side of Chicago and growing up in a home that had heavenly and demonic forces fighting over me and trying to exert influence over my parents, as well as their relatives and friends.

However, God always has His edge and His plan involved in our lives, and as much as it is required, He will employ what is necessary to accomplish what He wants done on Earth through us.

Chapter 3:
First Steps

"Can a woman forget her nursing child, and not have compassion on the son of her womb? Surely they may forget, yet I will not forget you." Isaiah 49:15

I grew up as a sick little boy who was constantly going to the doctor because of anemia, which was the result of being born too early and not being formed correctly. A lot of children in the world are born with many handicaps, terrible diseases, or horrible situations and circumstances because of what the enemy has endeavored to do through their families and relatives. However, God always intercepts the enemy with His powers and supernatural abilities.

I was the firstborn of three boys and one girl. During the first two years of my life, my father was always angry and upset with me every time he walked inside the house. He did not like the fact that I was born, and I always felt rejection from him. It was probably because the demon of selfishness controlled my father and made him think that I took away the attention he normally got from my mother. There was also the pressure and guilt that came from the reality that my parents conceived me before they were married, and that opened portals for the demons and allowed them to get involved.

During the first year after I was born, the angels had to watch over me very carefully, as they always do, to determine to what degree they could get involved, and to what degree the enemy and his demons were involved. The demons hit my parents with financial problems and fears of how they could make it on so little money. The South Side of Chicago was a very dangerous place, yet they were familiar with it. But fear was everywhere – in their minds and in their hearts. There was also guilt because Jesus had not yet been allowed to cleanse their hearts from these traces of evil. The enemy was putting all sorts of thoughts in their minds, filling their hearts and souls with his evil schemes.

When I was at the stage of still trying to walk and crawl, my parents were encouraging and appreciating my efforts. I would get up, try to walk, fall down and try again, doing what my parents were telling me to do. I would hear things like, *"You can do it!"* But my father would sometimes say things like, "Look at him, he can't walk right. He tries but he doesn't look like he's a normal kid. Maybe there's something wrong with him." This caused negative feelings to come upon me, but I kept trying to please my father. My mother would say, "He just has to keep trying, that's all." She was also trying to teach me words like "mama", "daddy", and others. Like any little child, I had some toys that I got from my mother and other family members, and even though these weren't expensive ones, I was happy in my own little world.

My mother couldn't understand why my father would say that he loved me and then push me away, or kiss me and then say, "Get away from me," stating that he was too busy. My father was putting expectations on me that I wasn't even ready for, so I would start to cry because I only wanted love, comfort, and encouragement. I wanted to hear him say, "That's a good boy. Look at how he does this.

Look at how he does that!" How wonderful it would have been if my father had treated me that way!

When I was alone, the angels would fill me with God's love and feelings of happiness which would well up on the inside of me, making me feel comfortable with the Holy Spirit always being around. The demons would watch to see how they could get involved, as they always do in the lives of humans. They access humans through their souls which, like with spokes in a wheel, have connections with their eyes, ears, feelings, desires, images, thoughts, and words.

My mother used to try and create a somewhat nice atmosphere in the house by listening to music via the city radio station that everyone listened to. However, the popular songs of the day being played on the little transistor radio were just another area through which the demonic world would try to get into my family's lives. There are songs that can fill the home's atmosphere with either negative or positive influences through the lyrics. People should be aware that the songs they listen to influence their thoughts. So, if a song is about love, it comes from Heaven, but if it is about selfishness and lust, it comes from the demonic powers with the intent to charm, as well as cause fear, breakups, and suffering. All you have to do is look at the lyrics of the song, and you will see what it projects to the listener. The demons come with the projection as you listen to those words, and the music charms you into believing and wanting or not wanting what the lyrics say. If it's a spell or a charm, it brings the desired or undesired results out of the pain that the singer is suffering from or wanting to express and get paid money for it.

Surprise, Surprise!

My parents wanted a color television for our home, but at that point they couldn't afford it. They used to argue back and forth on how they would be able to afford living in their own apartment.

Then my mother got pregnant with another baby when I was two years of age. Her thoughts were filled with panic about having another child with one little boy already and how she would be able to give enough attention to me, her firstborn.

As time went by, they did get a TV, and now there were shows that the entire family could watch, which filled our home with a different atmosphere.

Some of those TV shows that we watched I really enjoyed, just like some of the songs that my mother would play from the radio. Then another boy was born in our family, my little brother. He was a healthy boy, with no complications or health issues. My father worked during the day, and my mother took care of us. At times, she would need to take us to a relative's house or get a babysitter to watch us. When my mother started working at a factory and selling cosmetics through Avon, she would get some of her young female relatives to babysit us. I liked it because I would get to go with my mother to all those cool places and be around new people or other children.

When my baby brother was born, I noticed that my father favored him more than me. He would put me down and encourage my brother, for the demons were speaking to my father. They were putting thoughts inside his head, which he thought were his own. He thought that my brother was his favorite and that I would be my mother's favorite. My mother would at times say, "They're both your children!" But he would talk more to my brother and love him, and no matter what I tried to do to please him, it just wasn't good enough for him. Anything done by my brother was the most fantastic thing that a little boy could do, which made me feel very bad on the inside. Thoughts from the demons began to fill me and transform into questions like, *"Why does my daddy treat me this way?"* I wondered why I couldn't do anything right; maybe there was something wrong with me; maybe I just didn't fit into this world. My mother tried her best to love me, but all these negative thoughts would constantly come over me. Every time I would try to receive love, I would feel rejection or hear, "Get away from me, I don't want you!" or "You never do anything right!" Even in the later years, the discipline came for no reason at all – not just spankings, but slaps in the face and screaming at me inches from the face, with demonic looks coming off of my father. Harsh responses and discipline would be dealt out, even for little things like working on a model or playing with toys. As I grew up, I could never please my father, but my brother easily kept him happy, no matter what he did. This hurt me a lot, and I wondered why my brother was so special. Since I was the firstborn, my father would make me responsible for everything my brother would do. If anything would go wrong,

I got the blame, and the result was spanking and cruel treatment from my father.

"Fathers, do not embitter your children, or they will become discouraged." Colossians 3:21, New International Version (NIV)

Life Goes On

When I was six years old, another boy was born, the third child in our family. The baby was okay, although our family struggled to make ends meet. My parents were also trying to learn how to live in the world with their children. They would get advice on how to raise a family from those people that they knew. It was a very difficult time for my family because lack was everywhere. However, the angels were always ready to get involved whenever they could in our home. As soon as they could get in and bring influence from the heavenly realm, they would. There were periods of times when the finances would become better, or there was not as much trouble from friends or relatives getting involved with things that we dealt with. Life seemed normal, with my brothers getting all the love and care from our parents. We did what normal families do; the kids watched TV while our mother was busy, or we got to go with her when she visited relatives, while our father worked during the day. On the other side, the spiritual side, the angels watched, and the demons schemed while we lived our mundane, ordinary lives.

Chapter 4:
First Grade Trouble Begins

"Even if my father and mother abandon me, the Lord will hold me close."

Psalm 27:10, New Living Translation (NLT)

The day came for me to go to kindergarten and meet other little boys and girls, as well as my first teacher. The mothers would go with their children to drop them off at school, but some of us cried because we did not want to leave home. All the children were used to their families and homes, and now were uncomfortable with a foreign atmosphere. Some of the mothers would stay around a little bit to see how it went before they left to go back home and leave the children in the care of the teachers. The kids were introduced to toys and songs while the teachers played the piano. All the children loved listening to the nice teachers, drinking chocolate flavored or regular milk, and eating treats afterwards. At this point, the anxiety and fears from the new environment would leave as the teachers provided an atmosphere that the children loved and felt comfortable with.

Each day now began in school, and as all little children do when they feel comfortable, kids in my class started talking to each other and getting close to one another so they could play together. This one little girl and I got very close, and we discovered secret places in kindergarten where we could play with the blocks and the toys. We used to play house and pretend that we were husband and wife or the father and mother of a little baby, so we would take our milk with cookies and feed the family. We loved each other in the way that little children do when they play. The angels looked at us with delight and enjoyed how we would play in a make-believe, pretend world. Believe it or not, at that age, we had a little puppy love and got closer and closer to each other every single day. Even when the nurse would come to school, and we would have to get our shots, she would run up to me, give me a kiss, say it's going to be okay, and hug me. She pretended like I was her husband, and it made me feel really good, so I wanted to play and pretend that we were married. The rest of the children would also be doing whatever they did, but as long as everyone was playing and learning their lessons, the teacher was happy.

We sang our songs, did our skits and had fun. School activities were slowly taking over our little minds, and we thought it would go on like that forever. But going from kindergarten to first grade would change it all. My life was about to make a drastic turn because of what the demons of the neighborhood and the South Side of Chicago were planning. They were silently scheming while the angels were ready to intervene and come against the various things that they planned to do. It was God's plan for the angels to overcome the demons and to make sure that I made it through all the evil in my life. God watched with them, and waited and looked with pleasure. He knew that one day this child would receive His Son as a young man, follow His plan and be with Him forever, conquering all of his enemies and putting them under his feet.

Broken Home

When kindergarten was over, my mother and my father talked about how I would be going to the first grade after summer, and that I better enjoy that summer before school started in September. They mentioned that I would meet new kids, and it wouldn't be the same as it used to be. My dad was picking on me like a big bully and saying, "Just wait until you get in the first grade; you'll see how hard life really is." I thought, "Why, he sure has it in for me," not knowing what I was really thinking. The demonic powers were putting those thoughts in my mind, and then the next thought that came to my mind was, *"Your dad doesn't love you; your mother tries to protect you, but he really doesn't like you, he likes your brothers."* The demons would continually bother and harass me, and my father would slap me, yell at me, and say, "What's wrong with you, don't you listen? What is the matter with this kid? He does not understand anything I try to tell him. He'll never become anything in his life."

Believe me, these demonic spirits that would come out of his mouth would harass me and make me feel like I didn't want to live. Even in the first grade, I could never do anything right; it seemed that there was something wrong with me, and I constantly had this thought, *"Why is the world the way it is?"* It seemed that the atmosphere in our home was oppressive, extremely depressing and full of violence because of my father. On top of that, my parents used to always fight back and forth. I would see my mother try to smack him with an iron, and he would be smacking her back. Their background was from the rough streets, and their behavior was influenced by the gang of kids from their neighborhood. They grew up fighting quite a bit, swearing and spitting profanities, so these words consistently flowed out of my parents' mouths. As a result, I grew up with a tremendous amount of fear because everything was unsettling, even when I was just dealing with everyday life. Some things that I went through were normal for my dysfunctional family, but in reality, were the exact opposite of normal family life. I would get beaten for no reason at all, punched, or spit on for not being able to do what my father wanted me to do, even if it was just a little thing. It seemed he hated me, and when I tried to go to sleep, the demons would appear in the house, and I would see them. I would hide under the covers in terror, looking at what they were doing and yet, there was a curiosity in me to see what they looked like and how they would be communicating and talking to one another and to me. My brothers would feel it too as they were growing up.

The Trouble Begins

The time came for my mother to take me to school, introduce me to the new first grade teacher, and then leave me with the rest of the students. My first-grade class seemed normal for the first few weeks. Then the bullies and the troublemakers showed up – those who wanted to let everyone see that they were more special than others in the class. Life began to get very difficult at this point, and I did not transition into first grade well. I asked myself, *"Why am I trying to learn if I can't even understand what the teacher is saying?"* I sincerely tried, but there were no more toys to play with like in kindergarten, and so I had to stay all day in school like most children. We would have two recesses; one in the morning, then a lunch, then the second recess in the afternoon. That's where the interaction between the students happened. The kids that were there began to cause the demonic forces that were in them to come out, and believe me, a lot of what was in the children was caused by a demonic influence from their older siblings and families. I had a sweet little spirit, and I liked to talk to people if I could. It started okay, but then things changed with a lot of talk about how bad the neighborhood was and how cool they were. It was a big thing to those first graders if they could end up in a gang, just like their older brothers and sisters. These children followed in the footsteps of their families and became involved in crime to show how tough or bad they were, so that other people would look up to them. They believed that the stronger would rule over the weaker, and those who didn't want to fight were in trouble. Those who did not know how to fight or refused to fight would really get hurt.

Even at that early age, these kids were already motivated, mean, and dangerous because they learned all those traits from their brothers and sisters. There were established gangs in the area. This was also true for every neighborhood of Chicago, ever since different tribes of people came to the city from all over the world. Some people were quite interesting, and so they brought their culture and their religion with them. Most of the people in my area were Roman Catholics, and from their standpoint, you had to go to church because we had what was called catechism during the week. We had to go to church on Wednesdays to hear the Roman Catholic priest preach. Most people followed the tradition, but that was all they did; it really didn't mean anything to them. People went to church, and yet they acted the same way when they came out.

I have seen it throughout all my life, and it often reminded me of some of the born-again churches as well, which is so sad because we have a relationship with the Creator: God the Father, Jesus the Son, and the Holy Spirit. As Christians, we should start taking on His characteristics and His nature, and bring it into our world through what we say, based on what's on the inside of us. God's world has such love, wonder, and beauty. This world, on the other hand, has rulers of darkness and spiritual wickedness in high places that control people's minds, hearts, and wills to a degree that people let them into their lives through many doors – even through religion.

So, as I went to school every day, I learned to recognize immediately who were the tough and dangerous people, and I would try to stay away from them because I didn't want to be with them. They picked up on my avoidance tactics, and as bullies do, they began to pick on me, talk about me, and harass me, and it seemed that they enjoyed the company of their demons and partnered with them. They told me how stupid I was, which was similar to what I heard at home, and how I was a punk and a sissy. They began to push me around physically; they would laugh and tell jokes about me that they made up, and that made the whole room laugh at me. I didn't want to hurt anyone or to say bad things because I remembered that one time when they were beating me up outside; that was the day when I, being a little boy, had a wonderful vision of Jesus Christ for the first time in my life.

"Punch Him, Kick Him, Knock Him Out!"

They smacked my glasses so they went flying off my face; they started pushing me into the brick walls of the school building, smacking me, picking me up and punching me continually until I was bleeding and in a lot of pain. That's when I saw a vision of Jesus Christ dying on the cross for me, and it was what gave me comfort while all of that was still going on. Even though I didn't understand it, I learned in the Catholic Church that Jesus died on the cross for all of us. I needed the comfort because even when I was getting beaten, and the girlfriend I loved was screaming, "Punch him, kick him, knock him out," and I didn't want to hurt anyone.

The angels gave me the ability to see both the good and the evil simultaneously: Jesus dying on the cross for me in a vision and the demons and the kids laughing at me. This went on for years; I was constantly getting beaten up, going home and getting beaten up again by my dad, so it seemed there was no place for me in this world. I began to think that maybe I was different; maybe I didn't belong here. When I would go to my relatives during the week, my uncles would pick on me, say things about me that I did not like, and constantly harass me. They would say my name in weird ways that made me feel unwelcome. This was at my grandfather's home with two wives and over 20 children. Besides that, I also saw sex and incest everywhere, along with drinking, smoking, stealing, and everyone doing whatever they wanted to do. I wondered what kind of a world this was, or if there was something in me that made me a stranger here. The angels were probably trying to communicate to me that those were the demons that were making me feel like I didn't belong in the world, or that I was different than these so-called "normal" people. The demons had planned the course of my life from the very beginning, and now they were conditioning me for the future. Later in life, I was abducted by an enemy aircraft when I served in the military; I also became a sorcerer and a Satanist in subsequent years, so the demons seemed to be in control and progressively implement additional strategies to bring even more evil into my world.

While I was in school, the angels were continually trying to communicate to me that even though the world was a very bad place, I had to keep going. Something in me felt the encouragement from the angels, but I couldn't understand why I was treated so badly at home, at school, and in the neighborhood. I would think, *"Why did my life become like this?"* I would come home, and my father would pick on me and put me down every time he had a chance. He never encouraged me, never strengthened me, but used whatever things that I thought I was doing well to say, "You're stupid, you never do anything right, and you never do anything that I say. You don't hear what I say, what's wrong with you?" My mother would say, "He will learn, give him time." My father would reply, "Look at his brothers! They don't act like him. There is something wrong with him." Then he would beat me because I never did what he wanted, or I could never be good in his eyes or do anything that he expected me to do; he seemed to always have a good excuse to hurt me. I suffered a lot of abuse as a child because he did not know any better.

"Be kind to one another, tenderhearted, forgiving one another, even as God in Christ forgave you."

Ephesians 4:32

Now, as a believer, God had me forgive my father, and he came to Jesus Christ before he passed away. Because my father gave his life to Jesus Christ, he is now in Heaven, and I asked God to clean his slate and take away all of those things that he did to me. I forgave and released him from all those words, those punches, and the pain and the misery that I suffered from his physical beatings. Kids at school used to call me "potato head" because I had so many lumps all the time when I would try to hide from him. Then, again, those kids would pick on me and start hitting me, hurting me, pulling me around, and beating me up constantly – until things escalated when I got into the fourth grade.

Chapter 5:
My Childhood: Gang Intimidation, Manipulation, and Control

"My son, if sinners entice thee, consent thou not. If they say, Come with us, let us lay wait for blood, let us lurk privily for the innocent without the cause... walk thou not in the way with them; refrain thy foot from their path: for their feet run to evil, and make haste to shed blood." Proverbs 1:10-11, 15-16, King James Version (KJV)

There was one boy in my neighborhood that was supposedly a super tough guy. He gathered around himself a gang of other nine-year-old children who were walking around the streets after school with pipes, bats, and bottles. They acted like they owned the neighborhood along with their older brothers and sisters, and so they would come up to my brothers and me as we would play out in the street during the weekend and start smacking us around. They would tell us, "You're going to join us, or we will show you terrible things that we will do to you. You're going to fight and learn the way we do things. We rule this neighborhood, and we are the supreme power here." These were little kids acting cruelly and wickedly, swearing and cussing like they had a faucet pouring out evil words from their mouths. The demons would pour those words out of them to attack us so that my brothers and I would feel terror and fear. We tried to play alone in the streets, on the pavement in front of our apartment building, and a lot of times we were forced to run up to our apartment and hide when these kids came around. They brought a lot of fear with them, and even when we went to school, we would meet them, and because of their cruelty, beatings and intimidation continued.

One time they beat a boy down the street, and he ended up in the hospital because they beat him with a spiked bat. His name was Opa, and he had to join the gang when he got out of the hospital, or else they would have killed him. We had no choice; we had to join as well because so many children were already in the gang that it literally controlled the area. Becoming gang members was the only way out for my brothers and me. We had to go through what they called "the initiation process" of their organization where we would basically get beaten up. I got beaten up a lot more than the other kids because I didn't want to fight back. I refused to fight, so they made me the boy who would come down and bring the weapons when they had gang fights. I was sick to my stomach because of my involvement in the violence since I knew it was wrong, but I had no other choice. Our parents were not aware that we would go to the park down the street not to play, but to hang out with the gang from the neighborhood. The other gangs would come down from the tracks to fight, and they would use guns and shoot at us. I will never forget when I saw someone get shot in the middle of the fight, and how this person went down. I threw up at the sight of it, but I had to keep giving the weapons to those who were fighting. This was my life during school up until the seventh grade. Things gradually got tougher and more difficult as I grew older, and I thought I would get killed many times during one of the fights.

During that time, I met a guy who, for some reason, liked me even though he was a bit strange. I don't want to get into a lot of details, but he must've had some kind of a mental disorder; yet he protected me at times. To give you one example of this, we were one day at a large park, playing near the swing set when some gang members came up to us, and one of them pulled a knife on me. My friend ran up to us, kicked the knife out of the gangster's hand, and beat him up. I was so happy he did that! He also protected me one time from getting beaten up, but they hurt him badly for doing that. The thing is, he wasn't always around, but he became a good friend of mine when we got older. I even knew his sister and his mother, and I used to go to their home to play. They were a wonderful Puerto Rican and Mexican family, and I liked visiting them whenever I could. We played Mexican bingo and enjoyed the delicious foods that the family would bring to us as we played. They were always cooking something, and the dishes were delicious. His sisters were fun to play with, and we enjoyed our time with them, while outside the house people were getting shot and killed. One boy got killed right next door, so the family would always tell me to be careful when walking outside because the gangs were having wars again. I knew that, and because I was a part of a certain gang, I used to have to run through gangways or places in between homes to get away from some dangerous people who were driving around.

I was still getting picked on and beaten up at school. I wanted to fight my offenders, but something in me felt that it was a bad thing to do, so I refused. Even my uncles told me that I had to fight back, and they would pick on me until I tried to fight them because they said that I had to do it; that I couldn't be a water boy for a gang forever. I didn't want to be in a gang in the first place, but I had no choice. When I came home, I would hear my parents screaming and continuously cussing at each other. I did try to ignore them and just watch TV, but most of the time I stayed outside when I could. This is just how life was when you lived on the South Side of Chicago.

It was such a big thing to even be a part of a gang – at least that's the way the school kids looked at it. The demons enjoyed it because it gave people, even kids, arrogance, pride, and cruelty, and much suffering and pain to those whom they intimidated, controlled, hurt, wounded, and bruised.

When God showed me my past life in retrospect, I saw that the angels were continually trying to work in supernatural ways and protect the children from getting killed or being at the wrong place at the wrong time. The angels were trying to prevent situations where kids would get in the way of disgruntled gang members cussing their way as they were walking and wanting to pick on anyone they met. The heavenly guardians did all they could to protect the little girls from getting raped, which happened a lot – even to 9-year-olds or 10-year-olds. Of course, the pressure to have sex at a young age was a big thing because gang members thought that to be a tough and powerful person in that world, they had to have control over everyone – and that included their sex life. It is so sad that nobody would stop or hinder someone from doing awful things to those children living on the South Side of Chicago. I remember one good little girl who died of a head injury. I couldn't understand how an innocent girl like that could die such a horrific death. I also remember a little boy getting smacked in the head with a snowball that had glass in it. He also died. From time to time, even the gang members would die from fighting with each other.

Between Good and Evil

As I grew older, I saw death and suffering everywhere. The only time that I was able to get some peace was when my grandfather on my father's side asked me to go downtown and work with him on weekend mornings. I would work with him on the 18th floor of the Stevens building in downtown Chicago. It was called *"The Eleanor Club for Women."* This was my time to enjoy downtown and get to know all about it. My grandfather and I were treated very well, and we used to go to the 8th floor to have lunch. I would visit different floors, and soon I knew all the people who were operating the elevators and other people on those floors. I became friends with one woman who took a liking to me. She was a tea leaf reader and also read zodiac signs. When I think about her now, I feel certain that she was a witch. She used to say that I would grow up to be someone very special, and she taught me a little bit about the occult world. The demons were very happy that I connected with someone like that because their plan was to make me a sorcerer in the occult world, as well as to have me join Satanism and become a part of the Church of Satan.

I was also introduced to the world of pornography and especially *Playboy* because that was a big thing at the time. Even though I didn't understand it, I got influenced into buying and reading it. I found out that almost all other kids at school were doing the same thing. As a young boy, I dreaded older women because something terrible happened to me when I was younger. Ever since then, I had very bad sexual dreams plaguing me whenever I would go to sleep – up until the day when I was saved. However, God showed me later that the angels always tried their best to protect me, even from those bad dreams.

There were a lot of instances in my life when I felt that the angels saved me from harm. There was a time when I took my wagon and papers for a paper route in my neighborhood when a little tornado came by and scattered my papers all over the place, but I didn't get thrown in the air. It was a miracle, and I remember it way too well.

I used to go across the street to play and visit my childhood sweetheart. I would do anything for her. I remember how one time we were playing a ball game, and the ball went into the street. She pushed me, and when I ran, a car went by, and I was almost crushed underneath the vehicle. But the angels miraculously kept that car from running over me. It ripped my clothes really bad because when she pushed me, I went flying into the street. I slid underneath that vehicle and just kept my body down as it rolled over me. I believe the angels prevented that vehicle from squashing and killing me. A lot of days went by like that where I would go through different situations that could have caused me to have an injury, but I always miraculously escaped from getting hurt.

One Christmas, I was going down the stairs of the apartment building where I lived, and the store next door had a beautiful nativity scene in the window. It immediately grabbed my attention. Every winter since that day I used to stare at it and listen to the songs as much as I could, though it was very cold outside. I could almost feel God's presence, and the angels were delighted in what I was doing. It felt good, and I loved to stay there. I was also an altar boy for the Catholic Church, and my priest came up to me one day and said, "You're a very special little boy. One day, you're going to be a priest." Even though I didn't know what that was about, these experiences seemed very special to me. As I got older, I started taking care of the bread and wine for the priest with the other altar boys, and some of us would drink the wine but wouldn't eat the bread. We always made sure to drink the wine before the priest blessed it and not afterwards because we were taught it became the blood of Jesus. We would be in charge of those things for the communion service, and for some reason that was a peaceful thing for me to do. I got to hang out with the priest at times and was able to confess my sins, and he would teach me how to pray and what to pray for. I enjoyed spending time with the priest; I didn't even have to go into the confessional booth because he would let me tell him about my sins openly. That was a privilege of being an altar boy in our church, and I liked being on the good side of things with the priest. The other boys were getting into all kinds of mischief, but not me. Being in that extremely religious atmosphere was an interesting experience for me.

I met a young boy who lived across the street from my girlfriend – the same girl that I met when I was in kindergarten, whom I liked a lot and even loved as a little boy could love. He was into witchcraft, and that made me curious, so he took me to the little shed that he had near his house. The smells were horrible, and I felt like there was something terribly fearful in that shed. This boy couldn't be more than 11 or 12 years old, but even at that young age he was deep into witchcraft. Even though I didn't understand it very well, we ended up putting spells together, mixing potions, and calling on spirits to do his bidding. I felt that something was very wrong, and being there was bad for me, and I was in fear. I didn't want to disrupt what he was doing and saying, or give him the idea that I wasn't supporting him or believing in him, for I was afraid of what might happen to me if I did.

"There shall not be found among you anyone... who practices witchcraft, or a soothsayer, or one who interprets omens, or a sorcerer, or one who conjures spells, or a medium, or a spiritist, or one who calls up the dead. For all who do these things are an abomination to the Lord..." Deuteronomy 18:10-12

(Bitter)Sweet Childhood Memories

With that said, I do remember some good things about my childhood. We used to live next to a stockyard, and we would ride our bikes and watch the cattle coming off the trains before they got killed. We even watched pigs running for their lives and people trying to catch them, and that was pretty entertaining for us at that point. Down the street from the stockyard, the circus would come in once in a while. One time, we saw *The Beatles* drive by in their vehicle, with people screaming and yelling and women chasing the vehicle. I sometimes visited the cookie factory down the street and delighted myself in eating some of the cookies that got broken. There were many things that went on over at the local amphitheater, and I usually tried to look around and see what was going on there. I always kept my distance, but curiosity made me want to see what was happening. It was fun, and I believe the angels also wanted me to enjoy some simple things and were always around to protect me.

When I had extra money that I earned from working downtown with my grandfather, I would go into the dime store and look around or even buy some things. I also tried to help my parents, and I would go to the store to buy them food. I had a generous heart and wanted to bless everyone in my family, even though they treated me so badly. It made me feel good when I provided things for them. As I got older, I worked outside of stores asking people to carry their bags and thus earned some money. When Christmas time came around, I had money saved to buy everyone in my family little gifts, to bless them, and to make them happy. It would be a small gift, as small as something that would only cost 50 cents to a dollar. I had a lot of people to buy for, but it was cool to watch them open their little presents at Christmas time. It was so wonderful to see their eyes, and they all loved me during the holidays, but I was still picked on and messed with at other times. My grandfather greatly loved me; my grandmother didn't say much, but she would often hug me, so I knew she loved me too. My grandfather had two wives, and between them they had twenty-something children of different ages who were all growing up, so it was really difficult to keep them in line. I often stayed at their house and could see the terrible things that were happening every day in those children's lives.

I had to learn how to cook because when my father and mother were working, I was responsible for all the other kids. When my father got displeased, feeling that I did not do what he wanted me to do, he would beat me up. Sometimes his hands would swell from missing me and hitting the wall with his punches.

I went through that a lot during my childhood, so, needless to say, when pictures were taken, even of celebrations, I wasn't happy to be in photographs. I didn't like my life or being around my family when I was growing up. I always wanted to be with my grandfathers because they both treated me well. I would often hear my grandfather on my father's side say that honesty was the best policy, and that you should be honest in everything you do. Those were beautiful words that he said to me and that gave me a great memory of him. My other grandfather would beat up anyone who would try to pick on me. His voice alone would make people petrified with terror, and many chairs were broken over people's backs when he became angry. He was always drinking; cigarettes were everywhere, and even the babies that were born in his family had liquor in their bottles to put them to sleep or to help them during teething.

Our family became like a little gang, and anyone who messed with a family member would get in trouble. I often felt protected from my adversaries outside of our home, but at the same time I would get picked on a lot and called names by my own family members.

Even with having some love in my life from my grandfathers, the evil still outweighed the good, especially because of my father and the way he treated me, as well as the other family members who picked on me and called me names. Most people that I encountered bullied me and made me feel that I had no place in this world. Demons of vengeance were working overtime to make me feel that one day I would be able to show my true capabilities to everyone who hurt me and spoke against me. Those demons told me that even my parents, family, and peers from school would wish they had never hurt me or messed with me. I got bitter and angry more and more every day. And as the bitterness and anger progressed, I began having visions of what I would become and what I would do to those who had harmed me.

"See to it that no one falls short of the grace of God and that no bitter root grows up to cause trouble and defile many." Hebrews 12:15,
New International Version (NIV)

There were also times when angels would come, and I would feel the presence of God around me in a special way; but even that confused me because it did not mix with what I was normally feeling. Vengeance and violence had become a way of life for me. I was sure that one day I would make everyone respect me and pay for what they had done. The demons of vengeance and violence were so happy, and they were joining with many other demons and people controlled by them to make my life hell on Earth.

Life in the Hood

There were very dangerous people in the neighborhood – or the hood, as we called it – that hurt me all the time. I could've gotten killed many times, but the angels rescued and delivered me from those situations. It was a good thing that our apartment wasn't too far from the school, so I could run home as quickly as possible to make sure that none of the gang members would see me. And then, when I did get home, my father who was full of demons or, as the world would say, had a mental disorder and was dysfunctional, would cause me much pain and suffering from continually beating me and putting me down, saying that I was nothing and would never amount to anything. No confidence whatsoever would come from my father to encourage me to do anything. If I had a question, I would be smacked across the room. Or if I didn't understand something, the demon in him would say, "What's wrong with you, can't you understand anything? You can't do one thing that I say, and you always make a mistake in anything that I tell you to do. What's the matter with you?" He also treated my mother that way but he never did that to my brothers – only to me. I thought for a long time that, perhaps, there was something wrong with me, and I was not a normal person. I didn't look at things normally like everyone else and people hurt me all the time. The "poor old me" thoughts came to me continually, and I thought these were my own, but later God showed me it was the demons putting thoughts into my mind.

One time my parents had to go somewhere, leaving me home alone. I was alone and afraid, so I prayed to God. As I looked out of the window on the far side of my building, I said, "Please help me." All of a sudden, it was like I was surrounded by a cocoon of God's presence, His power and love. I felt comforted and knew the angels were right there, strengthening and helping me to endure the fear, just like they did many times when I was in gang fights, trying to be careful and not to get killed. I could feel the presence and comfort of the angels who would protect me even when someone would try to jump me in some parks outside of the neighborhood. They also protected me while I was in downtown Chicago with my grandfather; this is why being downtown became a place of relief for me during those years. It was a very confusing way to live – experiencing such evil and yet being protected by the angels and feeling God's presence. However, things were about to change quickly, for my family was about to move to another area.

Chapter 6:
Moving to a New School and New Area – Trouble Even Worse Than Before Begins

"For I said in my haste,

"I am cut off from before Your eyes";

Nevertheless You heard the voice of my supplications

When I cried out to You."

Psalm 31:22

When I was in sixth grade, my father and mother sat down with my brothers and myself and told us that we were getting ready to move to the Southwest Side of Chicago. My parents explained that we might end up owning a house, for they were going to rent with an option to buy. My dad said we would have to fix it up, which basically meant that I was going to have to help them. I was not looking forward to it because I knew my dad will be cussing and swearing all the time, with profane language pouring out of his mouth like a river, even if we moved to the happiest place on the planet. At that time, I got really depressed, and God showed to me later that it was because the demons were making me feel as if everything that was happening in my life would hurt me in some way. Many times, I would go by myself after such talks with my parents and cry or be very upset with what happened. The demons would just pounce on me with their evil words and feelings to make me wish that I've never lived on the face of the Earth. Then the demons of vengeance and violence would say, "You'll get back at them all soon, don't worry."

The day came when we moved, even though I did not want to go. My brothers and I had to share a room because the house needed a lot of work – even in the basement where I would end up living later. I also had to go to another school. Unfortunately, this school also had a gang, and I saw the markings of their territory on the walls of the school. As I saw the boys playing basketball and their girlfriends watching from a distance, I knew that I would have to avoid them because they were all members of the gang. I was getting ready to enter into seventh grade, and the first week of school, even the first month, was pretty good. I was learning and getting to know the students who were in my class, but since I was new, they had to figure me out by testing me, joking around, and such. When the bullies started in on me, the gang members were watching for my response to figure me out and size me up. After that period, people started picking on me again, beating me up, and so on. Even the girls would tear the hair out of my head because they wanted to show me how good they were at beating up people, or how strong and cruel they could be to people who were not like them. I used to go into a state that almost looked like a meditation, thinking that I'll get back at them one day; that I'll show them what I'm capable of. The pain was unbearable; the hurt and the bruises, both physical and emotional, were intolerable. I was wondering if I would survive this world or, perhaps, get killed like the rest of the people back in my old neighborhood. It seemed like it was always the good people who got killed; at that point, I didn't understand why the bad people survived instead.

One thing I could do well in school was dance. My art class teacher was also a music teacher, and we used to do dances. They said I danced like Elvis, and it was so cool because finally I did something that everybody liked, which made me feel good on the inside. The angels gave me wave after wave of good feelings, but then my talent for dancing also made some students very angry at me because I was better than them. Kids can be spiteful and do very bad things to you when they think they can push you around, bully and hurt you day after day with their words and with their punches. They can cause you great suffering with their actions and make you feel like there is no way out.

My life seemed to be nothing but suffering. I suffered at home while trying to help my dad fix our new house. He would yell and scream at me and tell me constantly that I was stupid, that I couldn't do anything right, that I couldn't understand anything, and so he would end up beating me every time. It seemed that there was no way out for me, and the demons made me feel so helpless and depressed. I didn't understand suicide, so I never thought of it at the time. I just wished I never lived; I felt like I never wanted to be a part of this planet. I would have these visions like I was someone else outside of this world, and I would connect to it sometimes without even knowing what I was doing.

Our new house on the Southwest Side of Chicago

An Encounter That Changed Everything

One day, just after I turned thirteen years old, I was walking down the street and suddenly ran into the members of a gang who had their leader with them. It was one of the biggest organizations in

Chicago that originated from 18th Street and had a branch at 38th Street. This person was the president of that organization, as well as the high priest of Satan worshippers from the local Satanic Church. He took one look at me and said, "Follow me, and I will make you the evilest person in this city. I will train and teach you, and you will serve Satan." He said, "You're going to go through the most gruesome training to be one of the worst persons in this city, and I'm going to give you supernatural powers that you can use to hurt, kill, and annihilate all your enemies." That's what I call being straightforward with a complete stranger! The key phrase that got my attention was when he said, *"You will* get back at everyone who has ever hurt you, and *you will* show them who you really are inside."

I was impressed by their gang colors that looked really cool and their sweaters that were not just to keep them warm, but also played the role of their flag. It was like they were from another country, walking in the enemy's territory, and I was shocked, amazed, and blown away that this person knew some of the thoughts that I carried with me for many years. So, I left everything, ran away from home and began to follow him, hoping to eventually become as evil as he was, if not worse. When I joined the Satanic Church and his gang organization, I was loyal, committed, and as dedicated as he said I would be, and they immediately started training me how to fight. I got beat up so many times that I have lost count, but then they gave me the demonic powers to fight back. The demons would blend with me and give me the knowledge of martial arts of all kinds, and I began to know how to do things in certain ways to hurt my opponents. I would be able to predict the moves of my enemies before they even did anything. I wound up learning how to hurt people, and the leader of the gang enjoyed it, even though one day I almost broke his back. He was ecstatic that I was being trained by the demons and by him, and loved the fact that he was able to identify my potential. He molded and shaped me into a fighting machine, with strong demonic powers that made me insane and utterly fearless. They would take me down to the different places on 18th Street and do certain things to train me on what to do when somebody had a gun pointed at me or was trying to kill me. Many times, it would seem that I could escape situations with bullets flying at me from different directions, or was able to do certain things that made it look like the demons had to be there. I could get out of those situations, hide in the midst of a crowd, and nobody would even see me, for if they did, they would've killed me. I had a Satanic discernment and a keen understanding of people even in our own group – I knew almost immediately if they could do very bad things to other people or not.

A Brand-New Season

During our meetings, we would have many blood sacrifices, and the women would be naked. We would put curses on people, and they would die in horrible ways, for we had the ability to use the power of witchcraft and black magic. We used the demonic powers to discipline gang members, so they would beat up those members to death, then at the end of the meeting heal or even resurrect them. We used drugs of all kinds and also sold them to make money. We lured young women to our meetings and put them in a trance, so they would do whatever we wanted. There were many things beyond imagination that happened inside the Satanic Church and our gang organization which I cannot talk about in this book.

Those were the evil people that I lived and worked with when I ran away from home. We would party all night – smoke, drink, use drugs, and then sleep during the day. Everything was committed and dedicated to Satan. Everywhere we went, we engaged in Satanic activities and were given over to our love for Satan. I felt that this way of life was what I was meant to do; that it made me into who I really was. I thought that my mission on Earth was to make everyone pay for my past hurts and show them that this is who I was, and that I could be exactly who Satan wanted me to become in this city.

The high priest became like a father to me, and he treated me like his son because he saw a vision of me. Little did I know that my high priest would also become a heroin addict, so watching him tie his arms and go through the horrors that he went through gave me a lot of pain, for I worshipped him as much as I worshipped Satan. I used to say, "Hail Satan!" to anyone who walked in my door, for in those days he was my god. I was delivered by my high priest from a life of suffering and constant beatings, so at some point I was able to walk back into my family's house and beat my father for all the times when he beat me. I took his car and rammed it up a light post, then stole his other vehicles and did whatever I wanted with them. As soon as I walked into any place where he was, I would immediately start a fight with him as a way of exacting revenge and getting back at him.

When school resumed, no one was willing to mess with me anymore because I wore my gang colors and didn't care what people thought. If anyone messed with me, they would also have to deal with my organization and with the demons and Satan. I could get into lots of details about those events, but then this book would be similar to numerous Hollywood movies about black magic – the worst kind of activity that has made many former light beings do very evil things here on Earth. However, there was one meeting that particularly stands out and relates to my conversion that I would like to mention.

I remember very clearly how one night we were all gathered in a circle, calling on the demons to appear. We could see these demons with our eyes opened or closed, for they were both physically and spiritually present in most of our meetings. This time, they appeared physically, and I heard the high priest speaking, commanding the demons to take my soul. All of a sudden, I felt the presence and saw the demon as it reached into me; I felt the grip of that demonic spirit as it grabbed me. Right then and there, a thought came to my mind, *"God, don't let them do it."* Then, the brightest light that anyone could ever imagine came in that circle and slammed it with such power that all the demons ran in terror and left everybody knocked down. No one knew what happened, and I don't know why I even had that thought, but I bet it was an angel putting heavenly thoughts into me and getting me to agree with him, and I did. Obviously, the enemy already had me at that time, but I was delivered in that particular moment. I don't know what would've happened if the demon succeeded in taking my soul. That meeting and experience was so powerful that I didn't even understand what had happened, but it didn't stop me from being who I was or what I was doing.

There's a scripture in the Gospel of John that says that the darkness cannot comprehend or understand the light. Our high priest got confused with what had happened, so he had all the members watching me very carefully to see if I carried any powers other than witchcraft. I obviously was very powerful, and the high priest became afraid of me because he couldn't take my powers, as with other members of the gang. Witchcraft came naturally to me – this was in part because of my family line. I was born with abilities and gifts because of my dad's mother who practiced the occult. Everyone would say I was a natural in the power of witchcraft, and I was completely committed and dedicated to Satan at that time. I tapped into some evil things and practices that I cannot write about in this book, but you can imagine the type of life that I lived.

The demons took us places and transferred us to all sorts of spiritual dimensions. There are supernatural layers, levels, or as we called them, *"planes of existence"* or *"realms"*, where the demonic powers controlled the time, the day and the week, as well as all other areas within the spiritual dimensions that were and still are under their control. There were hundreds of the occult powers that we had to learn to operate and become proficient in. I came out of my body many times even when I was younger, but with the occult and the demonic powers at my disposal, I could do that so much better.

However, during that particular meeting God's light filled the place and conquered those demonic powers to prepare me for the salvation of Jesus

Christ, so that I could enter into a committed, loyal, and dedicated relationship with Jesus and His dear Father at a certain point in my life. All the angelic hosts that helped me with this process were dedicated to this sole purpose and wanted to bring me *from darkness to light.*

*"I saw... **a light from heaven**, above the brightness of the sun, shining round about me and them which journeyed with me."* Acts 26:13

The Days of Our Youth

When I finally came to see my relatives and my grandfather with his two wives, they were all excited about how much I had changed. I wouldn't take anything from anyone anymore, even when my uncles would mess with me and wanted me to fight them. I didn't care how big they were or what was going on for them in the natural realm. At this point, they were into drugs as well, and they liked it that I also had some drugs on me from time to time. We would have parties all night; drinking, playing cards, and sometimes going bowling. Then I would go back and forth between my family and the high priest and his gang.

When I was with the high priest and the gang, I got back into doing all the things that were required of me, including the hits that had to be done or luring, bewitching, and recruiting girls and boys to join us. We manipulated them to do exactly what we wanted them to do, and they did it.

The gang did not consist of just us, however. You have to understand that this organization was very well-known and one of the largest in Chicago. Some of the members were way older than us and had lived through the gang wars and killings that took place in previous years. There were numerous slaughters of enemies and rival gangs that had taken place, and our organization was notorious and reputed because of its participation in those events.

I had supernatural powers – the same ones that Genghis Khan used to conquer the world and become very powerful and dangerous. The demons would talk to me, and I would know things about other people that nobody told me. I would discern things before they would happen, and I would get a sensation that I needed to get out of somewhere or start moving, or I would know exactly what to do in some situations.

That's not to say that the angels did not protect me, for I'm sure that they did try to the degree that they could. There were many times when a flood of people was looking for me after a fight, a shooting or a killing, and I was hidden from them between buildings and in walls. We used to think that it was cool to be evil, use profane language, and take advantage of people and make them suffer. It gave us a sense of power over others and made us do even more bad things; it was like a drug that got into us and made us the worst, the meanest, the most evil and deceptive individuals in the city. And so, it went on from day to day, week to week, month to month, and year to year, with me getting worse and worse. Pretty soon, I started wanting to hurt and hate everyone, especially those who hurt me. I would spend all my free time driving around the city and looking for those people.

When you become a member of the Satanic Church, you become close to one another, like you *are* one blood, and that's the way we looked at it. For one member to hurt another member was like hurting your own body. You had to be loyal to one another and committed to Satan's work, and your focus was on that completely.

Then I met this guy at school who became my friend, and we began to do robberies together. We robbed homes, trains, businesses, and people, and for me that was what real fun looked like. One day, some people from our organization were at a shopping mall to sell drugs and such, and they came upon my friend. They tried to rip him off and threatened to tear his face off. One guy pulled a bottle out and wanted to break it over his face, but I stepped in between them and said, "You're not going to mess with my friend." Needless to say, they were shocked that a member of their own blood would say that to another member to protect someone who was not a gang member. It was always agreed that we would care nothing for outsiders, and that's normal in the Satanic order. So, when I stood up to protect my friend, they said that we would talk about it at the meeting, but I told them that they couldn't touch my friend anyway, and they would have to go through me to do that.

The high priest of the organization arrived, and they explained to him what was going on. They said that I didn't want the organization to take what was rightfully theirs to take. He said we would have a meeting about this when we got back to the hood, and then he looked at me with disdain and said we would have a kangaroo trial. I got furious and said, "How dare you speak to me like that?" I used profane language and walked away, but they couldn't touch me, for they knew that I had powers and I was trained to fight – maybe even better than them or the high priest. The high priest also knew that he was getting older, and he thought that I was aiming to be the leader of that organization. But in my mind, no one simply had the right to tell me what I could do or not do with my friend – not even my organization. If I protected anyone, they were in my care, and nobody had the right to take advantage of them. I was willing to protect an outsider who was not one of us, and that was a no-no in our organization. But what was I supposed to do? I couldn't let them crush my friend's face with a bottle, take all of his money, beat him to a pulp, or kill him because he was my friend. I just had it in me, even though I was not a Christian and did not know that the Word of God says:

"Open your mouth for the speechless, in the cause of all who are appointed to die." Proverbs 31:8

I was about to find out what would happen in the next meeting, but the leader caught pneumonia and almost died; he ended up almost losing a lung. I wound up going to the hospital and being with him day and night until he made it through. I was still committed and dedicated to him because he had become like a father to me. I still respected and honored him. After he got out of the hospital, the other gang members reminded him about what happened at the mall and how they wanted me dealt with for that situation based on the rules of our organization. He did not call that meeting because he knew I was with him in the hospital, even though he told me previously that I was going on trial for that incident with my friend. He was willing to let it go even when the other members were always hounding him because they wanted to see me pay for the way I treated them. Finally, he called the meeting and put me in the middle of the circle to have a trial, and they wanted to have me punished. And so, I fought them all the way down four flights of stairs, with all of them trying to beat me. They tried every way to get me, but I was too good for them. Mind you, those were the people who had hurt and killed others on more than one occasion, and I was just a kid! They chased me all the way out the door, but I managed to escape. They even tried to get to me again one day when they came to my house. As I was walking down the stairs, I saw them, and we started fighting again. This happened a lot of times afterwards, as the guys from the Denver branch of our organization would not give up trying to get to me. Finally, some of the guys went back to their state, and some gave up. I ended up leaving the organization because I did not want to go back after that incident.

After I left the organization and before I joined a new one, a demon from the old organization was assigned against me. I remember how a ghostly demon appeared in front of me in smoke and fire, and took the gift that was given to me. As the demon entered the room, I elevated into the air and stood up trying to escape, but the demon threw me down. Green slime was coming out of my hands and feet, and I lost a gift the occult had given me. However, I soon regained it, and to a worse extent than ever before.

Chapter 7:
Going to High School and Joining a New Gang

"Fret not thyself because of evildoers,

Neither be thou envious against

the workers of iniquity.

For they shall soon be cut down like the grass,

And wither as the green herb."

Psalm 37:1-2, King James Version (KJV)

School was starting in September, and I was going to Curie High, a segregated school in a new neighborhood that brought together people of all colors from all over the city together, which was amazing. Like for any new student, the first few days were pretty cool for me. I spent breaks at the lunchroom and enjoyed what they served, and I took the bus on my way home every single day when school was over. I even met a friend that I grew up with, and we immediately connected and talked a little bit about how the new school was so different from where we used to go. I would normally have gone to a school that was in or near my neighborhood, but I got chosen to attend the new school through a lottery.

Curie Metro High School in Chicago

During the first days, everyone was staring at each other and wondering about each other, while teachers were introducing themselves to us. We were also spending a majority of the time trying to find our classes and where we belonged. We were all walking around getting lost in this huge new school, trying to figure out where every class was located, and it was very confusing but fun. Pretty soon, however, everyone got settled, and the gang members raised their colors to show everyone who was who and what they were going to do about it.

Since I was from a different organization than the ones represented in the new school, I tried to lay low. I even wore a black sweater, which meant that even though I was a former gang member, I was not going to represent another gang to anyone, for I was neutral. I wanted to stay clear of certain people because if they recognized me, I would have a fight on my hands very quickly, or maybe even a shootout, since the gang members carried guns, knives, and drugs to school. The boys would have their girlfriends carry their goods for them unless they were stupid, for it was very easy to get caught by a school monitor. If you got caught, you would go down to the office where they put most gang members in separate areas to figure out what to do with them. They tried to figure out who was who, so like me, a lot of the members laid low for at least three or four weeks before they became very transparent about who they were and what they were looking to do there. They weren't there just to go to school; they were recruiters sent to enlist different people that they thought would be good for their organization, or to get a hold of the ones that wanted to become gang members. In that particular school there were plenty of wannabes who came from all over the city due to the segregation policies, as well as multiple gangs to choose from. Their members would usually hang out in groups in different areas of the school. At lunchtime, everybody would go to the sub shop across the street, the billiard place right next door, or the 80-lane bowling alley with 13 pool tables, 2 restaurants, and a banquet hall. The name of the place was *"Marzano's Miami Bowl."* The older guys from the neighborhood would hang out at the billiard place, and whoever wanted to shoot pool, play with pinball machines, or eat Italian bread with mozzarella and sauce would go and spend most of their free time there.

Marzano's Miami Bowl, Chicago

When you would walk outside of the bowling alley kitchen, you would see the gang members out there, staring at everybody, using profane language, talking and yelling at the girls as they walked by, playing and goofing around, looking like they were really tough, bad and cool. The older guys from the neighborhood were after the younger girls, which the girls obviously loved, and many of them hooked up. Many girls ended up living together with these guys and having babies. I don't think any of them got married, although they ended up getting pregnant, and some even got sexually transmitted diseases.

Despite all that, I was still excited to go to school, just like the rest of the kids. We were given homework and other activities that students were supposed to do. I didn't have a car yet, so I had to take the bus to get to my family's home. I always had to watch my back because my former organization was after me, and many times I had to run just to escape from them. There were also other times when I was forced to fight them when they came to my house.

Welcome to Chicago All-Stars Gang

I made friends with one guy at school, and he told me about the new gang that was made up of former members of other gangs. This resulted in the new gang having experts in every kind of martial arts and weapons – even ammunitions and bombs. There were experts at pickpocketing, marksmanship, knives, and special kinds of Chinese weapons, as well as wrestling and street fighting. Most of them left their former gangs, moved into the area and now lived near the school. Members of this organization were always looking for people who were neutral and wanted to see who they were, what were their skills, where they came from, and if they planned to join. He said it was a fantastic opportunity for anyone looking for drugs, drinking, parties, and sex because lots of girls loved to hang out with gang members and be their girlfriends.

He filled me in on what the new gang was up to and what they were doing, and how it was a great opportunity for me. He thought because of where I had come from and my training, as well as the knowledge and experience of being with one of the largest gangs in Chicago, it would be a good fit. However, at that point, I did not know any of the other members, just him. I was curious because it was a big thing to be a part of a gang and organized crime, and it made me feel like I was someone and belonged somewhere. Every single one of us wants to belong, even if it's difficult. I couldn't stand sports, and the only thing I was really good at back then was playing guitar and singing. I was trained by a teacher from *Bel Air Music Studios*, and I used some of my money to pay for my lessons. I got to meet people that were in other bands, such as the guys from *Styx*, who used to play in a basement near Midway Airport. For a while, I was also a part of the band called *Jet*, and it was fun. *Styx* were just really starting out, and they weren't there much, so we got a chance to use their basement. But the gang was still the biggest thing you could be a part of in your school because it gave you an opportunity to be around the toughest and meanest guys and girls. So, I thought that becoming a member of this new gang was a chance for me to use my knowledge, understanding, and expertise to help the organization improve. I knew how the gangs functioned and operated, and I was skilled in the warfare of the streets. I knew who's having wars and why, who's getting killed and why, who's the strongest or most powerful, and who's handling the greatest territory. I had already cut ties with the other organization and was really thinking about joining this new gang, but I knew that I would have to be very cautious.

Even when someone was booked into Cook County Jail and got locked up with about 40 different guys, they found out very quickly that every single one of those guys was either with this gang or that gang. Many gang leaders ran their organizations from the prison, and when someone got locked up and went to one of the areas in the prison, they were asked what organization they belonged to. The prison leadership could usually tell what group a person really came from, and they would put the person together with others from their group or organization. Of course, they couldn't put people together who were rivals, or else they would start killing each other the moment they came into contact.

So that guy from school became a good friend of mine in the short amount of time that I'd known him. After the first few months, the gangs started fighting; people had their hair set on fire, there were riots between the black and white people, and it became tough just to get through the day at school. I decided to get more information from my friend about this new organization to find out what gangs the members had come from. I was assessing whether I was going to be challenged because of the backgrounds of the other gang members, and if so, to what extent I would be challenged. My friend was also interested in robbing places just like I was, so we've talked about that subject a lot.

Around that time, I noticed one of the girls on the basketball team and immediately fell in love with her. I would spend time watching her play until she eventually noticed me. We became friends and really hit it off. I started going out with her, and we had lots of fun together. One day, she told me that she loved me too, and so she became my girlfriend.

Due to my background, I eventually decided to join my friend's organization. I came up to him and asked him to set up a meeting with them. Of course, I never told my new girlfriend about these thoughts because I felt that there was no need for her to know.

The Meeting with the Last Gang I Joined

The gang was having a meeting in a garage, and the leader, the subjects, and the wannabes were all there. The wannabes were showing what they can do, who they were, where they came from, what they wanted to achieve, and the leader determined whether they were a good fit for the organization. Many tried to get in and wound up getting battered. I was thinking, "Since this happened to some of these people who were from all over, what would happen to me, a former member of one of the largest gangs in the city?" I only listened and didn't say much; I just watched every move of the spokesman and the leader. The warlord stood by with the girls, and there were the normal activities going on all around: profanity, cussing, shouting, yelling, and screaming.

This was typical of an organization, for everybody was trying to be better than everyone else and used intimidation, manipulation, and control as much as they possibly could.

When it came time for me to step up, the spokesman asked who I was and who brought me. My friend told them who I was and why I was interested in becoming a part of this organization. The leader listened very carefully, especially when my friend mentioned my background. I just listened and tried to look bad and tough, waiting for a fight or anything that would take place. Then they asked me, "Why are you here?" I basically said, "You guys may benefit from having me in your organization," even though in reality I was cussing and swearing just like everybody else; almost every other word that came out of my mouth was profanity. The leader said he would think about it and mentioned an initiation as well. He also said I couldn't be hooked up with that other organization anymore, and I had to let them know everything about me in detail. I was told that I would have to submit to a trial to check what I could do. If they didn't like me, they would kill me because I came from a very dangerous organization, and they couldn't take any chances with me.

And so it began. That was the final gang and organized crime group that I would be a part of before I came into a relationship with Jesus Christ. Then one day I was finally invited to another meeting, and when I got there, one of the guys wouldn't let me in because he knew about my previous organization. He was swearing at my friend and asking why I was allowed to go there when I could easily kill them all. He did not believe that I wanted to join their organization and thought that I was there just to check what they were about and later send my own organization to kill them. Fortunately, someone saw reason and told them to give me a chance because almost everyone in this group came from other organizations, just like that guy who did not want to trust me. The guy finally put his pistol away, but not after warning the others that they'd better be sure about letting me in. I wanted to keep my own pistol, just in case he tried to do something to me, but we eventually put away all our weapons. I was able to safely return home after that meeting, which was a miracle, and I do believe that the angels got me out of that sticky situation again. The demons were very upset, for they knew there was one part of me that wanted to send my old group after them for even treating me like that, but then the other part thought that they may have been a pretty smart group to think before they trusted anyone. There have been lots of instances when members of one gang tried to infiltrate another, or many times girls would go out with guys from other gangs to get information out of them. It always ended up with them trying to tear each other into pieces or to set up a deal with them in some way and to cause other members to be killed. It was all about territory, so fear, terror, and killing were all over the streets, and none of those gang members were afraid to get their hands dirty. If someone got out of line, they got sliced up or ended up dead. Not to mention that the mafia was usually involved with a lot of these gangs because they ran the drugs and women in the streets. This is what the life in the big city was like; gambling was used in many instances to launder money, terrorize the innocent, take advantage of the little girls, support shady businesses, and make lots and lots of money.

Before long, I started to think about letting my girl know what I was doing. I tried to be with her whenever I could because she provided me with that emotional comfort, and I enjoyed kissing her. In between the meetings with my gang, I tried to enjoy her love and company as much as I could.

In our group, you could not miss even a single meeting, or else you would get beaten up. There were also trials and initiations, as well as various other things you would have to do. You would have to get tested in every area to see what your skills were, how smart you were, how good you were in a gang fight, and if you would stand up for the gang, their colors and the things that they stood for.

What I didn't know, however, was that my former organization had already heard about what I was doing, and they were furious. They were making plans to come down to the hood where I was living and kill me, even though after the last supernatural thing that happened in the meeting, no one wanted to mess with me. They didn't know what kind of power I had to cause that to take place, but they knew I was powerful. Despite all of this, the angels were still happily optimistic, for they knew that God would always protect and watch over me to make sure that I would come to know His Son for the eternity.

"And I give unto them eternal life; and they shall never perish, neither shall any man pluck them out of my hand." John 10:28, King James Version (KJV)

The Real Street Fighter

The time came when the gang finally recognized my efforts and admitted me as a full member of their organization. I had proven myself over and over again with the gruesome things that I had to go through. I finally got to proudly wear their colors, and they noticed how I enjoyed it and how loyal, committed, and dedicated I was to all that their organization was about. I wanted to see them become the largest gang in the city of Chicago. Maybe it was the demons, but there was something in me that wanted to become the leader of that organization one day. From battle to battle, from one thing to the next, I started getting known, and my name became respected and honored.

Marzano's Miami Bowl, Chicago

There was a time when I got into a fight in the bowling alley with a ton of gang members from another organization. They were after me and the colors that I wore, which represented my group. I had some of my guys walk out to get reinforcements, and some stay because there were around 30 rival gang members, and we wouldn't have time to run and would have to start fighting them; and so, we did, but we were outnumbered.

They finally cornered me, and one of their members, a Puerto Rican who was a martial arts expert, came into the circle. He knew they had me, but he decided that he wanted a one on one fight. He was very fast on his feet, and he hit me so bad a few times that I ended up bleeding and hurting. In my mind, I was wondering where my people were, but since they didn't seem to be coming, I had no choice but to fight back. I tried to trick him and pulled out a pipe, breaking his jaw. This move made the other members of his group take off at once.

My angels were glad to step in and help, and I know that for some reason the angels were the ones who caused that group to flee. I mean, there was no real reason for them to flee, for they didn't seem to be afraid of anyone, but the atmosphere shifted, and I could tell that something changed right there and then. I tried to gather my senses as best as I could, while they ran and took their fighter away. I finally found the guys from my group, and I was very angry at all of them. My girlfriend was there, and she immediately ran up to hold me and tried to find something to clean the blood off of me, crying at the bloody sight of me.

One of the leaders of our group came up to me and asked what happened, so I told him, and he said that our members were going to pay for it because they had left me in that situation. Everyone was shocked that I was still alive, for there were a lot of guys chasing after me, and they circled and fought me and the few other guys that I was with. That incident proved to my group that I was worthy of being their member, so they stopped testing and trying me. I had already proven to everyone what I could do for the gang.

After that fight the other members looked at me like a warrior and were proud to fight alongside me. It proved my commitment and loyalty to my organization, and that's what the president wanted at that time; it didn't matter how bad we got beaten up or who ended up in the hospital or died. His only question was, *"Did you fight for us?"* I said I broke the jaw of one of the members of that group and they took the guy away when they left. At that point, there was no more questioning me about who I was before because I became a full-fledged, honorable member of their organization.

That was just one of the highlights during the years that I was with them before giving my life to Jesus. My life was like the worst action movie you could imagine. Over the years I got gradually meaner and became very well-known in the organization, which ended up being backed by the mob. Of course, my former organization still tried a few times to set me up or kill me. The leader himself had a .357 Magnum, so on one occasion he jumped out of the vehicle and started shooting at me out in the street. I ran to him, which was crazy since he was shooting at me. The bullets never hit me, which by itself was another miracle, and I only realized later that the angels protected me again. They have done this many times throughout my life even though I was involved in organized crime. People who saw me said it was like the bullets went right through me when they saw me running after him.

I have to say there were some very unique things that happened to me, even though I cannot explain what exactly happened. There was a day when I was running across the street and a car hit me. Witnesses said it was like Superman got hit by a paper plane because I jumped on the car and landed onto the windshield, but I didn't stay there. I jumped off, ran into the bowling alley and went to sleep. When I woke up, everyone was saying I was like Superman out there and wondering how I did it, for they all saw what happened to me. Looking back, it seems that the angels saw me getting hit and obviously picked me up in such a way that when I got hit by the vehicle, I bounced off.

*"Because you **have made** the Lord...*

your dwelling place, no evil shall befall you,

Nor shall any plague come near your dwelling;

For He shall give His angels charge over you,

*To keep you in **all your ways**.*

In their hands they shall bear you up,

Lest you dash your foot against a stone."

Psalm 91:9-12

There were lots of incidents like this, such as when I was in gang fights down on 18th Street. Lots of people got killed there; some were stabbed or shot, but we were still continually going down there, as we were raising what we called a *"nation"*. The organization was growing very quickly, and other branches were developing in the other locations, so we were looking to take over the whole Southwest side of Chicago. We had to go around and show our strength because a new gang was also starting up, and some of the older gangs were starting to really come into our neighborhood. It was partly because the Mafia was throwing around lots of money and supplying gangs with weapons and drugs. In return, we did lots of things for the Mafia as well and protected their family members and others as directed. Even though I wasn't active in the Satanic church at the time, I could still see demons because of my background. And the atmosphere definitely got thicker with demons when the drugs and selling of women started en masse.

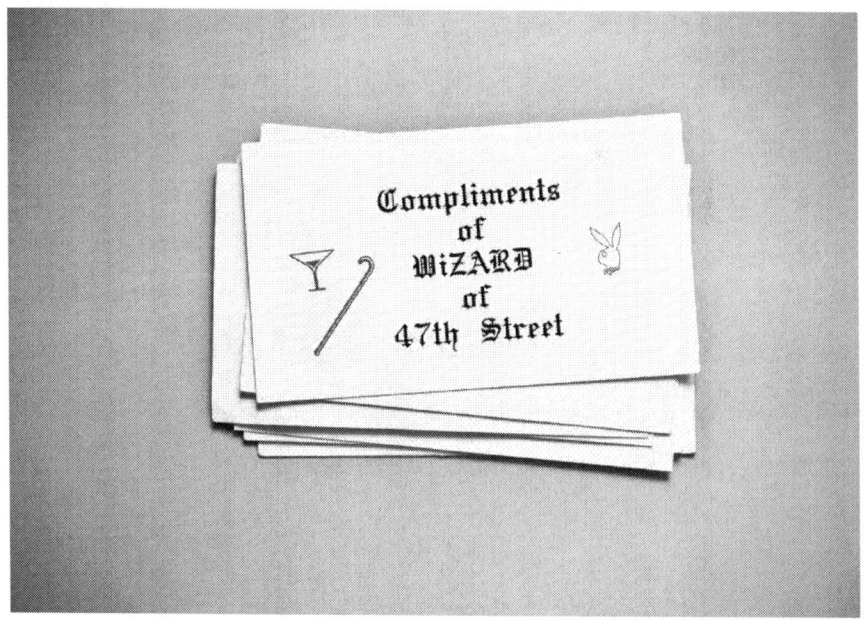

Business card of a gang member

We had tons of gang fights, and guys would be streaming through the gangways in between the houses to fight us and using all kinds of tricks, like blowing up our vehicles. We would start fights at school; we would go to various parks to fight other gangs; we had experts in various kinds of martial arts and weapons of all sorts. We even had our own Golden Gloves fighter. We also trained newer members and came to be known as *"the heavies"*, for we were the highest royalty, honored like generals in the military. We also had a large number of leaders with different skills and abilities who could take over branches, distribute the drugs, and handle the money, as well as the women that were the ladies of the night. Those days, girls would sell themselves in any way just to have the drugs that they wanted, and we had them all. There was lots of money coming in from different areas; besides that, we were ripping off houses, businesses, and trains, and we had lots of fences[1] to take care of the merchandise.

---

[1] "Dealers in stolen goods" in thieves' slang, middlemen between thieves and the eventual buyers of stolen goods.

Becoming a Gang Overlord

The demons were quietly rejoicing, and I became more committed than ever to turning our gang into the number one organization on the Southwest side of Chicago. I was completely taken over by this thought. Some looked at me and said I was one insane dude, for I did the craziest, most bizarre things that other members would never do. I was arrogant and confident because I knew my demonic allies were working overtime to protect me. We would go to other organizations, pull out our guns, and start shooting everybody we saw as soon as our cars stopped. A fight started everywhere we went. Pretty soon, I started carrying a sword in my cashmere coat. I had guns on me and a shotgun at times, and I was always protected by other members as needed. Our girls would carry some of the weapons and drugs, so if a gang crime unit came around, they would get away and leave us there. We would get busted, but they couldn't get us for anything. I escaped so many dangerous situations, and I even beat officers quite a few times, so I was a frequent visitor in jail. People got so committed and dedicated to me they called it an honor just to be locked up with me until the Mafia lawyers got me out of jail. Otherwise, we were very smart and learned how to stay out of prison.

Then I started having others do the crimes for me so I would come out clean, and the gang members were totally committed to me as their leader, even if they got locked up because of me. I was rising very quickly despite many horrifying situations, like people getting killed or women getting raped all around me. I didn't care because I knew our organization was going to be number one in the entire city. The violence would not stop and even escalated over time.

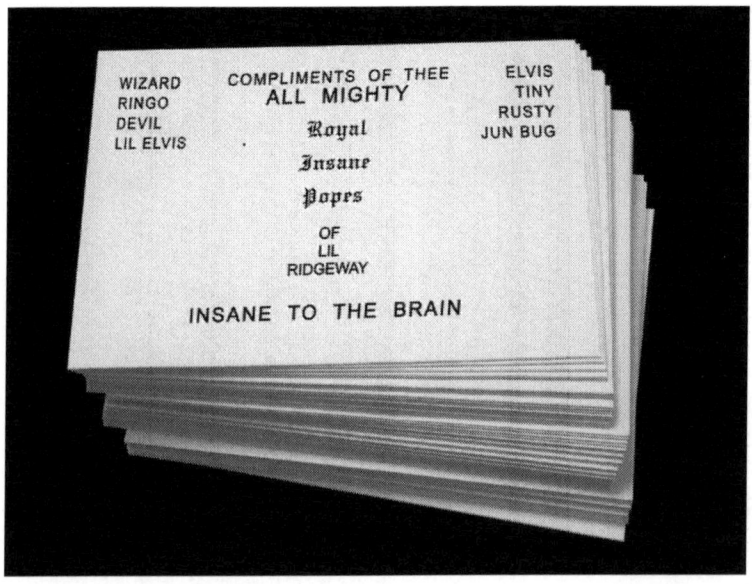

Business card representing several members of a gang

And yet, there was something in me that was so hard to explain. At times, I would feel the presence of God around me. I didn't understand it at the time, but now I do, for I know what it feels like to be in the presence of God. I'm sure the angels were protecting me when I was visited by demons that appeared like a black smoke in front of me and picked me up in the air. Angels were on their toes many times to protect me from the physical and spiritual attacks. There were also times when I would go back to my parents' house, and as soon as my father saw me, we would start fist fighting because of the anger and the bitterness that I felt for him. I wanted so bad to get back at him for all the pain and suffering he caused me. When I came to understand what Jesus did for me, I forgave him for all those things, and got rid of those bad feelings and harmful emotions at once. I knew that forgiveness was the key that, through the Lord Jesus Christ and His power, would set me free.

Chapter 8:
The Gangs Are All Here! The Beginning of Organized Crime

"Why do the nations rage,

And the people plot a vain thing?

The kings of the earth set themselves,

And the rulers take counsel together against the Lord..."

Psalm 2:1-2

I became very well-known in the neighborhood as someone very authoritative and powerful. I was feared because of my supernatural evil abilities and demonic protection over my life. The other gang leaders gave me a place as well, since we were getting organized and connected with various other leaders to sell drugs and with local fences to distribute stolen merchandise. The drugs came into our neighborhood with full force since they were brought in by the mob. There were also weapons of all kinds and soldiers coming back from Vietnam who were specialists in various areas, and they joined us and became very dedicated to the whole organization. We provided various levels of training for those who wanted to learn about fighting, martial arts, weapons, and surviving in the streets. Members who were talented in certain aspects taught other members how to take people out. A lot of wannabes came to us, including those who just got out of prison. We had fights and shootouts, and we dealt heroin, cocaine, angel dust (PCP), and acid (LSD). There were many kinds of demons that were associated with those drugs from the ancient times and connected through the worship of the ancient gods to the plants that drugs were created from. The demons controlled and influenced people through the drugs they used.

We live in a world that has been taken over by the Prince of Darkness. The demons and the territorial spirits that ruled the neighborhoods and the South Side of Chicago were so cruel that they could influence even the smallest children. You would see children taking advantage of others, being very cruel to each other, showing selfishness, and feeling that they were bigger and better than everyone else. They resorted to manipulation, intimidation, and fear that the demons planted in their minds. They schemed throughout all the neighborhoods of Chicago, as well as in various cities of the world.

Evil has spread out all over the planet, and you see it in meetings, political and religious regimes, and nations that fight others and terrorize those who cannot fight back. They all want to be number one and are driven by demonic forces that cannot be seen with the natural eyes.

What they don't realize, though, is that only Jesus should be the number one for all. He invites and welcomes people to come to Him just as they are, as long as they accept all that He has done on the cross. He wants to help us get away from the destruction that the demons have wrought in our lives. Jesus came to destroy the works of darkness. I've seen throughout the years of my life that it is true because Jesus has done His work in my life, even though I was a seemingly impossible project. It is okay if you're a difficult project; He can still handle you. You just have to let Him do it, and sometimes it's not easy, but He will help you once you take the first step. You will feel that nothing is impossible with God. He is the Creator of all things, and His spiritual energy will destroy every force that comes against us.

"He who sins is of the devil, for the devil has sinned from the beginning. For this purpose the Son of God was manifested, that He might destroy the works of the devil." 1 John 3:8

Protected by God's Angels

Gangs and organized crime in our city also used witchcraft. That was one of the reasons why I was recruited – because of my background in Satanism. They saw supernatural things that took place around me, especially since it seemed that no one could kill me.

There was one time when two police officers busted 22 people, but they couldn't get me. There were secret compartments within the walls inside the house, so I hid there for hours, and no one was able to find me. It would have been really bad if I was caught with those who got busted because the house was full of stolen merchandise and drugs. A lot of people who were there had warrants for their arrest or were known to be involved in criminal activities. I know that the angels were guiding and directing me not to get caught, for in that case I could've served seven years in prison. There were other times I could've gotten busted, but God sent the angels to protect me, and for some reason I got out of it miraculously. Because I was protected, I began to feel very powerful, and as we would walk down the street, people would say, "Here come the heavies," not meaning that I was overweight; it was a term that people used because we were the highest level of the criminal organization operating in our neighborhood.

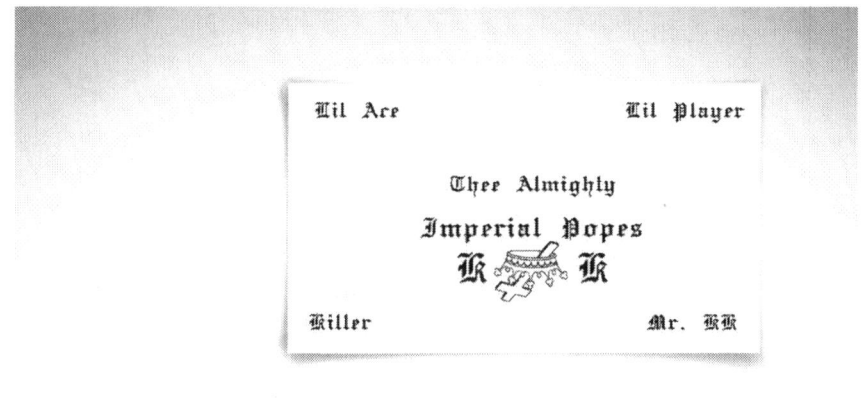

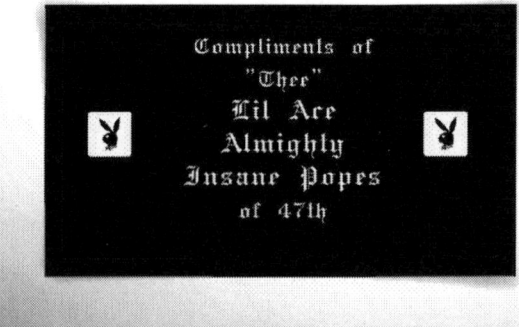

Business cards of Chicago gang members

Another example of me almost getting killed was when I did cocaine and heroin the night before a hit, and I wasn't quite prepared for what I had to do the next day. I could have made some pretty deep mistakes that could have caused us harm, so I told one of the leaders that I wouldn't go because I wasn't ready, and he understood. I believe the angels protected me again because a gun went off in the car right where I normally sat, and I would have been killed on the spot had I been there.

When jobs were assigned in the organization, there were usually three to four guys in the back of the car, and I sat in the middle with two more in the front seat. The special gang crimes division chased their car, and when they tried to get rid of their weapons, one of them by mistake tried to throw the sawed-off shotgun out of the window, forgetting in his panic that the window was not opened all the way. The result was that everyone inside the car got shot, and some lost their fingers. The officers who were chasing them thought they were shooting at the police, so they started shooting back, which caused the vehicle to crash. It was a very bad situation, and many people could have been killed, including pedestrians. If on that particular day I was sitting where I was supposed to, I would have taken the brunt of the shot and would have died. Most of them had to go to the hospital and some to jail. It was a miracle that no one from our group got killed. This showed me that the angels were looking out for me again, for they knew that one day I would receive Jesus Christ and all that He did for me. I would be a testimony of how cool and awesome God could be and how He could come through for people even if they didn't even know Him or were against any form of religion. When I went about my normal business that day, everyone who saw me was shocked because they thought I was with the group who had trouble with the police. Even my girl started crying and asking me if I was alright when she saw me. I told her I was fine and I didn't go on that hit because I was really wasted. I went into a café, ordered coffee, and sat down with my arm around my lady. I told everyone that I was fine and tried to find out who was in the hospital. One of my friends came in and told me what happened. It wasn't until many years later that I realized: the angels of the living God were protecting me all along.

Since some of the leaders ended up in prison or the hospital, I had to take charge and get lawyers to start the process of getting them out of prison. Then I got the other leaders of the origination together, and we had a meeting to discuss these events. We were fighting with other gangs, so we started making plans on who we needed to take down and who we needed to go after; we also discussed the events that led to the imprisonment of the other leaders. At that time, we were also involved with the

Nazi party when Tom Collins was their leader, and we had to attend a scheduled march by Marquette Park down Western Avenue. After the rally someone got shot; the National Guard was on riot patrol and started shooting everyone with rubber bullets, but we managed to take off.

...Time and Time Again

Another example of angels protecting me was when something went down on 18th Street. We were in a funeral home, paying respects to one of our members who got killed, when all of a sudden someone came up to us and said there were enemies outside. They started shooting, so all of us ran out of the building. Everybody had weapons, so we jumped into cars and started chasing them and trying to shoot them. We were furious that they would even come near us when we were paying respect to a former member who got killed. After a while, the cops got involved and started shooting at us too, trying to stop us because we were capping at the others, and many people could have ended up being shot in the streets. I could see the angels protecting us, putting shields up, and making sure that I didn't get shot, for they knew that very soon I would come to know God's Son, Jesus Christ.

I remember hiding because the police were looking for us, and at that point people were running everywhere, and it was getting dark as the sun went down. For some reason, right there and then I saw my life pass before me: everything I ever did, all the evil that I had in my life, seemed to scroll in front of my face. There was very little good there. I probably was in shock, and my heart was pounding, but this time something was taking place that wasn't normal. Why did my life pass before me? Looking back, I believe that it was a process of getting me ready to go before His throne because I started seeing more spiritual things again. I'm sure the angels were preparing me for my salvation and, slowly but surely, taking me from darkness to light so I could eventually begin walking in God's ways.

Our vehicles got confiscated, and I wound up taking a bus back to the hood. I remember getting off the bus and standing on 26th Street, trying to get back to my neighborhood when a carload of guys went by, and I could see that they were going to do something bad. They jumped out of their vehicles, but I was able to get away. That night, I made it back to my house, not knowing who got busted or who got shot from our group. We drew comfort from our girls and the music that we played; we spent the night smoking joints, trying to settle down and find out what was going on in the neighborhood. We needed to determine what to do next – if we were to go back down there with some other guys and avenge ourselves or not. We were thinking of the kind of strategy we could employ, and I came up with the idea of a suicide mission for the sole purpose of killing them all. I had vengeance on my mind that would not stop, so the plan was in the making, but God and His angels had other plans for me, and the best was yet to come.

Chapter 9:
The Last Week of Criminal Activity

*"God our Savior... desires **all** men to be saved and to come to the knowledge of the truth..."* 1 Timothy 2:3-4

Even though there was a whole bunch of criminal activities going on, there are only a few that I can write about in this book. This all happened before I came to know the Lord Jesus. I was on the run because the mob put a contract out on my life. The mob believed that I had killed the leader's son with drugs, but I didn't do it. He took too many drugs even when I told him not to, and when he was tripping, he jumped out of a window and later died in the hospital. Later, after I came to know the Lord, the mob found out that I didn't try to kill him, so the contract was lifted. My reputation was cleared; however, the people that told the mob that I had killed him got in trouble. Again, nothing but an angelic intervention has protected me. I bet the demons were just blown away by all the things that God did to get hold of me. They must've wondered how it could happen – how I could keep on escaping their schemes, for the enemy only wanted me to experience suffering, pain, and misery throughout my life and eternity.

When I came to know Jesus, I never went back – except for the times when God wanted me to speak to the gangs about what happened to me. Most people don't understand that once you come to realize your destiny is with God, you can't go back to where you were before. You *must* walk away from those things, even though your old connections do all they can to draw you back into it. God can send His angels, knock out the demonic forces, and keep you out of it, but you still need to exercise your will because you have to make the decision not go back to your old ways. That's where many people fail – because leaving their old life and walking with the Lord is their own decision to make, and they have to stand by it. I've seen many try to walk with the Lord, but they went back to their old life; someone tried to pull them back into darkness, and they did not resist.

During those last weeks that I was with the gang, I was planning the suicide mission and strategizing how to kill the members of other gangs that were causing all the trouble going on in our hood. I wasn't living at home with my parents at that time; I was sleeping in my vehicle outside my aunt's house in below zero weather. During severe storms, my aunt would let me into her apartment. Things were very bad for me because I was still on the run from the mob before they cancelled the contract on my life, and my aunt lived in my rival gang's area, so I had to be very careful when I walked around, drove around, or even showed my face.

One day I went to look for one of the gang members and found him at his mother's house. She was a born-again Christian, along with his grandfather. Even though they were a Christian family, all the kids were members in my gang. That Christian lady told us about a meeting held in our city by Vicki Jamison, a well-known evangelist, and said that she could heal people – even *me*. Her kids, my gang members, were afraid of me so much that they started joking and saying that going to that meeting would do me some good. They laughed and said that we could even case the place and figure out how to rob the people in the meeting. I don't even know why I said yes, but I decided to go – not knowing that it was all part of God's plan. I can only imagine how ecstatic those angels were at that point, rubbing their hands and saying, *"Finally God's plan is unfolding!"* They probably thought that at that point they had me all set, so they were reporting to Heaven, telling the others to get ready. They probably told the Father, *"This boy is coming to Your throne, and we are going to see to it that he has an experience of a lifetime and will come to know Your Son."*

The Lord can't wait for every single person on this planet to get to know His Son. His desire is to reveal to us how Adam and Eve came to be, what happened to them, how He gave the Ten Commandments to their descendants, and why Jesus had to die on the cross. He wants us to understand the spiritual sacrifice that Jesus made with His blood and not just to have head knowledge about His physical suffering. He wants us to be aware of the complete forgiveness available to every one of us for whatever we have done against Him.

"Wasn't it clearly predicted that the Messiah would have to suffer all these things before entering his glory?"

Luke 24:26, New Living Translation (NLT)

You see, this world, with all its influences and most of the thoughts, words, and expressions is only able to make people feel miserable. God's plan is that we would begin to live wonderful lives in Him where He helps us to think right, to speak right, and to do the things that are right. God never wanted the world to become like it is now. And He's going to change it in many ways very soon.

Baptized with Fire

I went to the meeting and walked in all full of pride, dressed to the hilt in my organization's colors. I remember that the evangelist had started the meeting already, and when we walked in, she said Jesus was there, and I thought, *"Where?"* I was brought up Roman Catholic and baptized in St. Augustine's Cathedral, which was a huge thing on the South Side of Chicago. I was also born in August, on the day when Mary ascended to Heaven, so my priest used to say to me when I was younger, *"You're going to be a special boy one day."* I did not understand what he meant. As the meeting continued, I looked around to see if I could find at least one statue of Mary that I got used to seeing at the Catholic Church. However, what I saw instead shook me to the core. When I looked up, I saw a cloud that was swirling in the air, and Vicki Jamison said that the glory of the Lord was present in that place. I kept staring at the cloud, and then she started pointing out at people and saying, "You're being healed in the wonderful name of Jesus." I saw that many people got healed right there in their seats, but all of a sudden, I started hearing the demons around me, shouting at me and telling me that I needed to get out, that I did not belong in there. The evangelist looked at the back row, pointed her finger at me, and said, "You're being healed right now in the wonderful name of Jesus." Suddenly something that felt like fire shot out of her fingers and right into me, and I felt like something was burning me. The fire spread and was burning all over my entire body. I kept seeing the clouds swirling around, but all I could do at that point was run out of the building. I was burning up from the inside, and little did I know that I had demons within me that were getting cast out, and right then and there I was getting healed deep inside. The demons were running for their lives from the fire and the wrath of God!

In the past, I used to go to the hospital, and they never could figure out what was wrong with me because I would start rolling around on the ground. I used to have some kind of a painful stomach disorder, and God completely healed me in that meeting. When I ran out of there, I noticed a cloud following me all the way into my car. I was trying to find ways to explain what was going on with me to my friends, but I couldn't. They immediately lit up joints because everyone was scared, probably even more than I was, and kept telling me that we should just get back to the hood. They were all afraid of what took place; later on, however, one of the friends told me he saw the cloud too. We went back to the hood, and I was flipping out so much over what had just happened that I kicked someone for something, and now everyone was looking at me like I was losing it. Even my friends who were with me in the car were saying I'd lost it at some point, and something had gone seriously wrong with me.

I got dropped off at the Christian mother's house. I needed to talk to her, and so I decided I wasn't going to leave until I figured out what was going on. I still felt the burning fire all over my body, and I didn't know what was happening. When I knocked on the door, I could tell she was praying in other languages, which she told me later was the result of the baptism in the Holy Spirit. She opened the door and asked me to come in, which was shocking because at that time I was considered a very dangerous person. I sat down, and she told me that I had to go back to the meeting. A weird feeling came over me; when she said that, the fire immediately transformed into a cooling sensation. It was like having thousands of comfy blankets wrapped around me and a soothing, refreshing sense of peace coming to comfort me. I could imagine the angels were wrapping me with comfort and giving me the feeling that it was going to be okay. The frenzy and fear all fled away from me in an instant, and I finally was at peace. I felt better than I had ever felt in my life; somehow, I knew that it was all going to be okay. She told me that I could sleep in her house that night, which was a miracle in itself; on top of that, that night I probably had the most wonderful sleep in my entire life. The demons were far away, and I could not even think of them – just the peace and the feeling of love and comfort throughout that whole night. The supernatural blanket of peace and love seemed to make me feel good all night long, and I woke up feeling the same wonderful comfort that I had never experienced before.

Chapter 10:
The Beginning of a New Life Never Lived Before!

*"Therefore, if anyone is in Christ, **he is** a new creation; old things have passed away; behold, all things have become new."* 2 Corinthians 5:17

The next day we had breakfast, and a Christian girl that happened to come over agreed to take me to the meeting. Everyone who was there assured me that I would be okay this time. I believed them because I was still feeling that beautiful sensation and comfort that I experienced the night before. And so, we went, and as I walked into the meeting this time, I was very peaceful and calm and felt very good overall. No one from my organization was with me – only that Christian girl who had taken me to the meeting. As we went towards our seats, I could feel that the demons inside of me were tied up and couldn't talk or communicate with me anymore. I just felt that powerful quietness and tranquility, instead of the demons making me feel like I was being dragged away from that place. We sat a little bit more towards the front of the room. As they were conducting the service, I was feeling so good and wondering what was going to happen next. I heard the evangelist say, "Some of you were here yesterday, and you came back today. You know exactly why you did that: you're here to make your stand before the Lord and give your lives to Him."

Suddenly a light brighter than the sun surrounded me, and I started to rise out of my seat. I could see almost right through the whole place; I found myself standing before the throne of the Heavenly Creator of all, God the Father. I felt like I was transported – whether in my body or out of my body, I'm not sure, but it happened. In that vision, I was standing before God the Father, and Jesus was right beside Him. It was like the Father was smiling at me. He almost looked human – so beautiful, but in a spiritual form, and He spoke joyfully to me. As He spoke to me, I saw the cross of Jesus, what He did for me throughout my entire life, and what He went through to make this meeting with the Father possible. I saw three visions as He welcomed me before His throne. He also showed me right then and there that He believed in me. No one ever believed in me before, and that is why I felt so wonderful, so absolutely happy; there was a total absence of terror and fear in that heavenly place.

In the first vision, I saw my life pass before me as if I had died. In the second vision, I saw my organization tied up like a bundle, and I knew it was about to be thrown into the fire, which I realized was the hellfire. I clearly saw my organization, my colors, and what we stood for. I was so committed and dedicated to all of that, and I vowed I would never leave it. Then the Lord spoke to me and said, "This is what I want you to do: I want you to leave that behind and come follow My Son; do what He tells you to do and learn about Him. Give up your organization and follow my Son Jesus, and I will help you. I will put My words in your mouth." I knew I had to do it, so I surrendered to His will. He put words into my mouth, and it seemed like there were billions of words and images going into me. I felt so wonderful, so peaceful, and there was such a good feeling surrounding me and a sensation of His love, which I never knew before. It felt so good to be there that I never wanted to leave. I wanted to be there forever, not realizing that's what He established and set up for all of us – to be with Him forever. By then, the light being within me had completely forgotten the wonderful worlds it originally came from. Little did I know that God could actually remind me about the pre-existent world and the inexplicable experience in all the levels, dimensions, and unfathomable ways of His power, majesty, and awesomeness.

I said, *"Yes, I will do it,"* not knowing what was going on in that meeting. I was totally taken in by the phenomenal energy, the power, the light, the beauty, and the knowledge of the fact that the Father of all creation loved me, and Jesus died for me and gave me the ability to be with Him forever. All I had to do was learn from Him and leave all of my old ways behind. That, however, was going to become the biggest challenge that I would face, and I was completely unaware of that at the time, but I simply felt His limitless power; His angels were with me, and I somehow felt that I could do it.

As I came back into my body, my hands went up, and something suddenly hit me, knocking me back into the aisle. This happened when the evangelist was giving what they said was an altar call, where people were asked to come out of their seats, come to the front and dedicate their lives to Jesus Christ. Vicky Jamison asked everyone in need of that prayer to go to the middle aisle, which I willingly did, with that brightness of God's love and light still surrounding me. As I went up front, I was talking to God and told Him, "I am Your project, and You have a big one on Your hands." I knew in my heart that God was letting me feel secure, that He had my back, and that the demons were no longer in control of my life. Vicky asked everyone to repeat the words that I clearly remember up until this day, *"Jesus, come into my life. I want You to come into my heart and become my Savior and my Lord. Forgive me of all my crimes and sins. I give my life to You. I dedicate my life completely to You."*

Suddenly, it started happening all over again – that feeling of the burning fire came back to me, and I sensed it deep on the inside. This time, however, it was accompanied by the love that I felt when I was in Heaven with God the Father. I knew very clearly that Jesus came into my heart, or the center of my being. Everything outside now looked different; every sound felt different, and then the evangelist said, *"Now that Jesus Christ is in your life, you can receive the baptism of the Holy Ghost."* I had no idea what that was, but I agreed, and she put her hands on me. The Holy Spirit, the Spirit of Most High God, flooded my being, and I began to speak in those other languages and could not stop for a long time. It was so cool, and from that point on I have constantly had visions and wonderful spiritual experiences throughout my entire Christian life.

In an instant, I was set free from so many demonic powers – like drugs, profanity, alcoholism, vengeance, and all the things of this world that held onto my life. I was free and I knew it. I felt like a bird released from the cage. My life was never the same again and never will be, for I gave my life to the supreme King of Kings and Lord of Lords, the Overcomer of all the spiritual forces of demons in the Satanic kingdom that kept me bound for years.

Most humans are bound to demons through their thoughts, expressions, words, songs, lies, deceptions, fears, and terrors and can never set themselves free. That's why they need Jesus, even though they don't even seem to know it. God had a wonderful plan for me, and Jesus set me free for a specific purpose. This was the beginning of a life transformed and my personal way from darkness to light. I wasn't aware of it at the time, but later on I found out that other gang members also gave their lives to the Lord and went down to the front of the building that night to say a prayer that would change their lives once and for all.

"Whoever calls on the name of the Lord shall be saved."
Acts 2:21

Things Will Never Be the Same Again

I went back to see the Christian lady who originally invited me to the meeting, and there were other Christians in her house who welcomed me into God's family, as they called it. They discussed what to do with me and said that they couldn't leave me alone because I had to literally get out of the area in order to make it and keep my new commitment to the Lord Jesus Christ. If I stayed in the city, I would be too weak and slide back into my old way of life. The question was where to put me.

One suggestion was to take me to a place called *Teen Challenge* the next day, so I stayed overnight.

The problem was, that *Teen Challenge* location was too close to where my enemies lived, and they would've loved to get hold of me, so that was not an option. The next day, I went to another Christian woman's house who told me that I could stay there temporarily until they figured out what to do with me. In the meantime, I could not stop praying in the beautiful languages of the Holy Spirit. I could hear angels singing with me, so they let me stay in a separate bedroom so I could remain caught up in the spiritual experiences. I never had such beautiful experiences before. It seemed that I was a brand-new creation on the inside, and even on the outside everything looked different and seemed to be filled with a beautiful light. I could hear the angels sing and rejoice even though I wasn't in church, and I had never felt like that before. It was so cool, so wonderful, and so fantastic!

"The wind blows where it wishes, and you hear the sound of it, but cannot tell where it comes from and where it goes. So is everyone who is born of the Spirit."
John 3:8

I had so many questions, and they told me to read the Bible. I could feel the covering of the angels around me and feel the protection and love of God surrounding me like a beautiful canopy. I felt so protected, so completely overwhelmed and thankful that He chose me to come into this kind of life. I was even excited to see what was coming up next in this new adventure, what could happen, and what kind of a quest this would be overall. I have never experienced anything quite as fantastic and wonderful as knowing and realizing that Jesus came into my being, and that He was there to stay.

The girl who took me to the meeting made a call to Minnesota to her mother who already had about eight teenagers of different ages living in her house. She said that she felt God was telling her to bring me up there. They prepared a small room for me and said that their family would take care of me until I could find a discipleship home to help me grow in Jesus Christ. It was not easy for me to trust her because my normal thoughts were so far different from this solution, but I chose to go, so we made plans. She already knew the trouble that could come my way if I stayed in Chicago. After a 10-hour trip, they welcomed me in their home. They also introduced me to my new church and some of the people there. It was a very large church right off of Hennepin Avenue in Minnesota.

After I unpacked my belongings, I couldn't stop reading the Bible; there was a hunger in me that made it feel like food that I was eating, even though I didn't understand a single word at that time. However, it was like some kind of a magical book to me, and the words seemed to really become alive and start filling me up as I was reading. Everyone I met said I was drinking the sincere milk of the Word, and God Himself was feeding me because I needed to grow. Jesus came into my life, and suddenly I was like a newborn baby all over again. That's exactly how I felt – like I was brand new inside and outside. My entire being was changed when those demons left me. I looked like a devil before, and now God made me look like an angel.

The family that sheltered me lived in the suburbs outside the city, and I would occasionally go out and take their German Shepherd for a walk. As we were walking, I couldn't stop praying. I'd either be talking to God or yelling at Him, asking Him questions or wondering what was going on in my new life with Him. I spent many days asking God all the questions that I could come up with. The host family seemed to love it that I was so thirsty for finding out more about my brand new Christian life, even though He Himself was the reason behind my new desires and habits. Jesus really does set people up to get into a position where they can receive Him. When the decision is made, He comes in and makes sure that the new child of God will have His angels and the Father, the Son, and His Precious Holy Spirit watching over them and taking care of them. I learned it was the first of many steps to take in my life, and the fascinating journey that can't be described in detail in one single book was only beginning...

One Last Thing Before We Close...

If anyone of you reading this book does not have a relationship with the Father, Jesus, or the Holy Spirit, all you have to do is ask. He is calling all those who want to come to Him. You can receive His salvation and be born again.

Just go into a quiet place and say, *"Heavenly Father, I want Your Son, Jesus, to come into my being and my life, to live in me, and to dwell in me like He did it for Tom. I ask that You forgive all my wrongs through the cross of Jesus Christ and cleanse me with His blood. Thank You for coming into my life and into my world. I believe that Jesus died for me on the cross, and now I'm granted access to live in Heaven with You forever. Thank You, dear Heavenly Father. Amen."*

If you just asked Him to come in, you are born from above. Now, you're a citizen of two worlds – Heaven and Earth. Now that He has come into your heart, you can begin to live your new life in Him. So simply begin studying the New Testament, and a good place to start would be with the Gospel of John. Get into a small group that believes the same things that this book explains, and you will get to learn more and prepare for your journey.

Welcome into the Kingdom of God! Your Heavenly Father, His Son Jesus, and the Holy Spirit love you.

*"For **you were once darkness, but now you are light** in the Lord. Walk as children of light."*

Ephesians 5:8

ABOUT THE AUTHOR

Tom was born and grew up on the South Side of Chicago. In his early teens, he became a runaway and joined his first gang. His involvement with the gang led him into a life of alcoholism, drugs, crime, Satan worship, witchcraft, and other forms of the occult. He pushed his way to the top and eventually became the president of one of the largest gangs in Chicago. Then, a dramatic life change came when Tom had a divine encounter with God. He was taken in the spirit before the throne of God and presented with a decision. He accepted Jesus into his heart and was commissioned by God to travel throughout the world presenting the Gospel in the spirit and power of Elijah.

Tom graduated from *Christ For The Nations Institute* with a degree in Practical Theology, and over the past 39 years he has traveled the world ministering to thousands of people in crusades, churches, correctional facilities, youth groups, youth homes, schools, seminars, and conferences. He has been ordained as a Prophet, is a psalmist and minstrel who invokes the presence of God, and flows in strong discernment of spirits, deliverance, impartation, wisdom, and revelation of the Lord. He has also consulted with law enforcement agencies on ritual abuse and gang crimes because of his background in the occult. He is a John Maxwell Certified Speaker, Coach, and Trainer. Currently Tom is enrolled at the *Israel Institute of Biblical Studies* where he learns ancient Biblical and modern Hebrew. Besides that, he ministers in the Washington State Benton-Franklin County Jail to inmates on a weekly basis.

Visit www.tomslone.com
for more information about
the author and the
upcoming books and
projects.

Made in the USA
San Bernardino, CA
26 July 2018